Gérard PALOQU

AEROBATIC TEAMS

Translated from the French by Sally Brown

HISTOIRE & COLLECTIONS

ARGENTINA

"Cruz del Sur"

In 1962, the *Fuerza Aerea Argentina* (FAA/Argentinean Air Force) celebrated its 50th anniversary and created the aerobatic display team "Cruz del Sur" (Southern Cross). One of the pilots of Grupo Aéreo 1 of Caza-Bombardeo of the IV Brigada Aérea based at El Plumerillo, in the province of Mendoza, was very experienced in flying the F-86F Sabre that had equipped the FAA since September 1960, and had the idea of creating an aerobatic air display team similar to those that existed at the time in Europe and North America. In 1962, eleven F-86F Sabres were given a bright livery of sky blue, red and yellow (the squadron colours) and the Southern Cross constellation on the tail fin. The squadron gave public displays all over the country, but was disbanded at the end of the same year. It was reformed in 1997, equipped this time with the Sukhoï Su-29AR with which it still flies under the name of "V Escuadrón Sukhoi", and is still with the IV Brigada Aérea díEl Plumerillo-Mendoza.

North American F-86F Sabre of the "Cruz del Sur" display team. *Fuerza Aerea Argentina* (Argentinean Air Force). El Plumerillo-Mendoza, 1962.

North American F-86F Sabre of the "Cruz del Sur" Second livery, 1962 (addition of red areas).

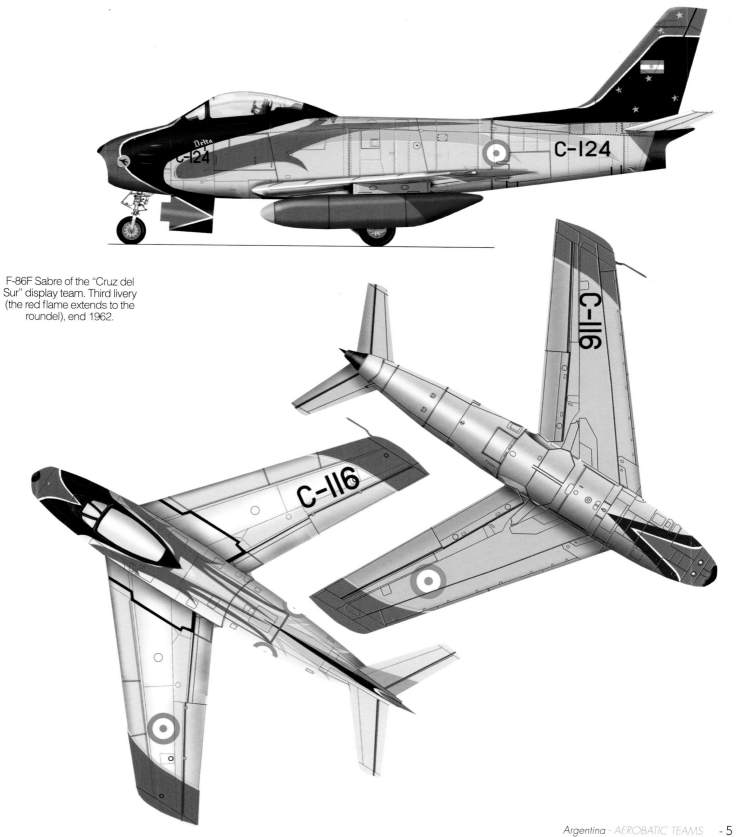

F-86F Sabre of the "Cruz del Sur" display team. Third livery (the red flame extends to the roundel), end 1962.

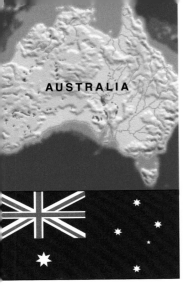

AUSTRALIA

"The Meteorites"

In 1952 and 1953, an aerobatic display team comprising of Gloster Meteor T.7 of the RAAF (Royal Australian Air Force) Central Flying School, the leader of which was a flying instructor, was the first to bear the name of the "The Meteorites", but it was disbanded at the end of 1953. This display team's aircraft bore no special livery.

The "Meteorites" were reformed in 1956, this time with three Gloster Meteor F.8 of the 78th Fighter Wing based at Williamstown, near Melbourne. This display team, led by Flight Lieutenant J. H. Flemming, carried out twenty-three displays and was disbanded in February 1957.

"The Telstars"

A new aerobatic display team named the "The Telstars" appeared in February 1963, equipped this time with the De Havilland 115 Vampire T35. It carried out its first display

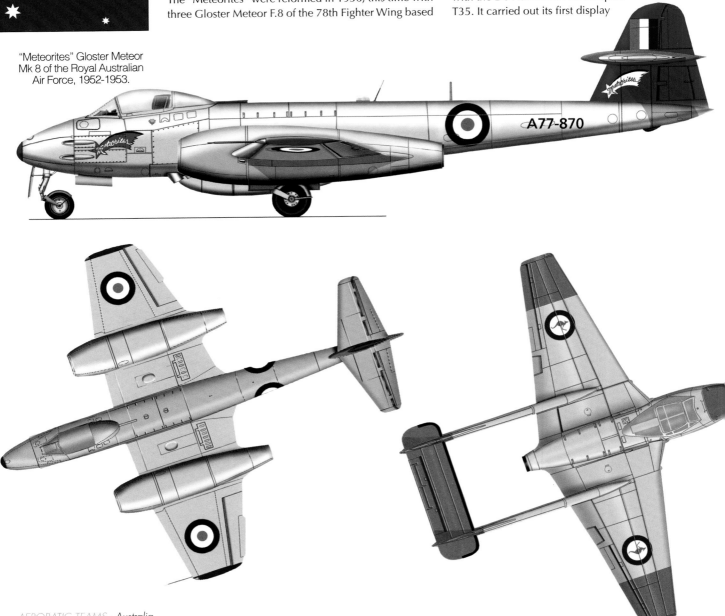

"Meteorites" Gloster Meteor Mk 8 of the Royal Australian Air Force, 1952-1953.

A77-870

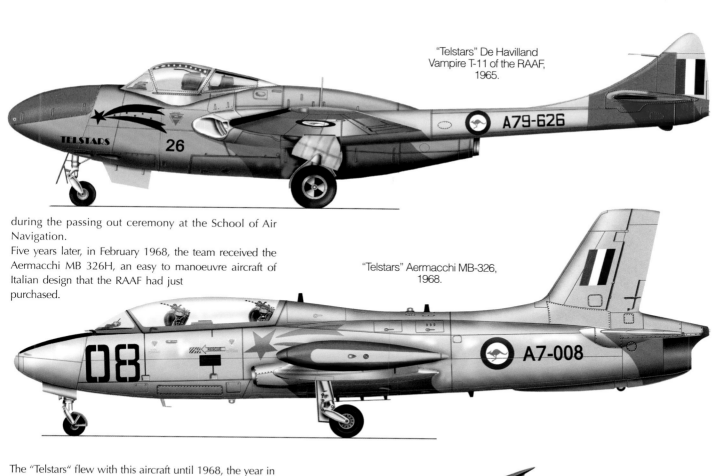

"Telstars" De Havilland Vampire T-11 of the RAAF, 1965.

A79-626

TELSTARS 26

during the passing out ceremony at the School of Air Navigation.

Five years later, in February 1968, the team received the Aermacchi MB 326H, an easy to manoeuvre aircraft of Italian design that the RAAF had just purchased.

"Telstars" Aermacchi MB-326, 1968.

08 A7-008

The "Telstars" flew with this aircraft until 1968, the year in which the display team was disbanded due to a large reduction of display flights by the RAAF.

"The Roulettes"

It was at Point Cook air base, near Melbourne, that the "Roulettes" carried out their first public display in December 1970, just before the Golden Anniversary of Australian air forces that took place the following year. At the beginning, this display team flew with four Aermacchi MB 326 and took its name from one of its most spectacular aerobatic manoeuvres, "the roulette".

The "Roulettes" carried out their first public display in March 1974 with five aircraft at the Point Cook air base, during the passing out ceremony for new officers of the Air Academy. The fifth aircraft flew solo and the formation of the other four aircraft separated into teams of two.

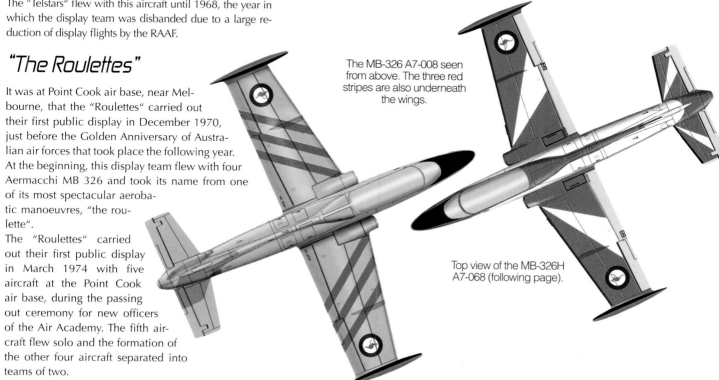

The MB-326 A7-008 seen from above. The three red stripes are also underneath the wings.

Top view of the MB-326H A7-068 (following page).

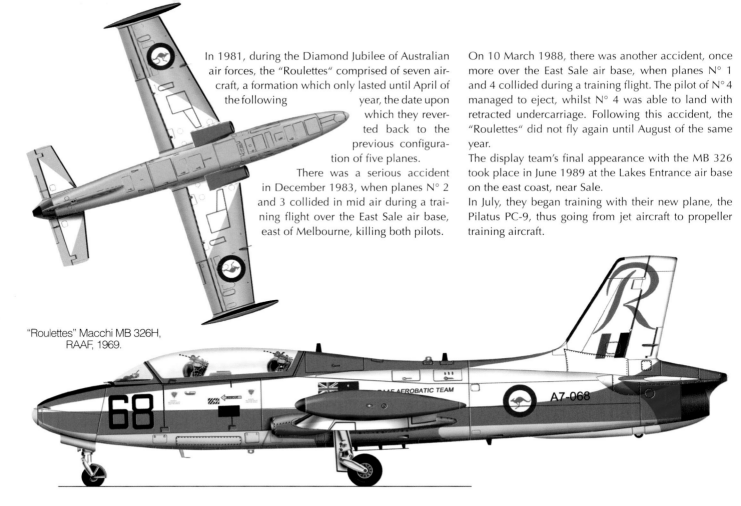

In 1981, during the Diamond Jubilee of Australian air forces, the "Roulettes" comprised of seven aircraft, a formation which only lasted until April of the following year, the date upon which they reverted back to the previous configuration of five planes.

There was a serious accident in December 1983, when planes N° 2 and 3 collided in mid air during a training flight over the East Sale air base, east of Melbourne, killing both pilots.

On 10 March 1988, there was another accident, once more over the East Sale air base, when planes N° 1 and 4 collided during a training flight. The pilot of N° 4 managed to eject, whilst N° 4 was able to land with retracted undercarriage. Following this accident, the "Roulettes" did not fly again until August of the same year.

The display team's final appearance with the MB 326 took place in June 1989 at the Lakes Entrance air base on the east coast, near Sale.

In July, they began training with their new plane, the Pilatus PC-9, thus going from jet aircraft to propeller training aircraft.

"Roulettes" Macchi MB 326H, RAAF, 1969.

AUSTRIA

"Karo As"

The first aerobatic display team was created in 1966 within the *Östereichische Luftstreitkräfte* (Austrian Air Force) was the "Silver Birds" and was equipped with four CM-170

Fouga Magister. Disbanded in 1968, this display team was reformed in 1975 at the Linz-Hörsching air base under the name of "Karo As" (ace of spades) and equipped with four SAAB 105Ö The "Karo As" were definitively disbanded in 1984.

"Karo As" SAAB 105Ö of the Östereichische Luftstreitkräfte (Austrian Air Force), 1978.

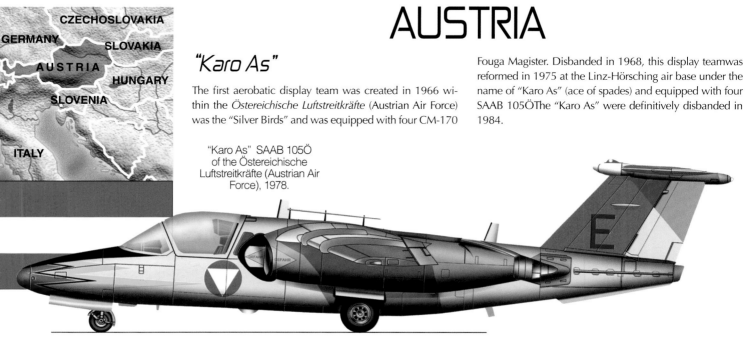

BELGIUM

"The Red Devils"

In 1957, following the disbanding of the "Acrobobs" that were formed within No 350 Squadron and which flew with four Gloster Meteor F.8, an aerobatic display team equipped with the Hawker Hunter F.6 was created within the 7th Fighter Wing of Chièvres. The new team, which had not yet been given a name, carried out its first public display in France at Valenciennes, on 12 June 1957.

On 10 octobre 1959, during the Chièvres air show, the display team comprised of nine aircraft, then sixteen a few weeks later at the Gosselies air show. The general staff of the *Force Aérienne Belge* (FAéB) decided that these large formations were too costly and the display team was later reduced to only four Hunters. The latter

were given a bright red livery and their number was increased to six with the addition of two replacement aircraft. It was at this point that the team was named the "Red Devils". The display team undertook its first display with this name in 1960, but was disbanded on 23 June 1963 after the Chièvres air show.

In 1965, the display teamwas reactivated, equipped this time with five Fouga Magister CM-170R which were also painted red. They carried out their first display on June 27 at Brustem.

After having their numbers decreased to two (1972), due the oil crisis of the nineteen-seventies, then increased to three (1973), the "Diables rouges" had to wait until 1974 before reaching their previous number, flying six Fouga Magisters, a number that they retained until they were disbanded in 1977.

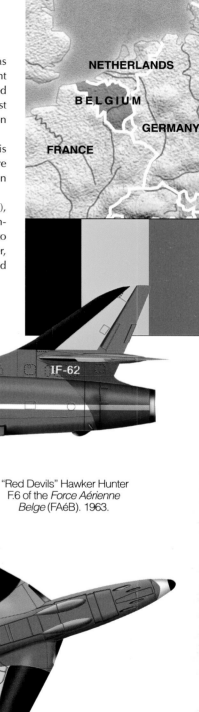

NETHERLANDS

BELGIUM

GERMANY

FRANCE

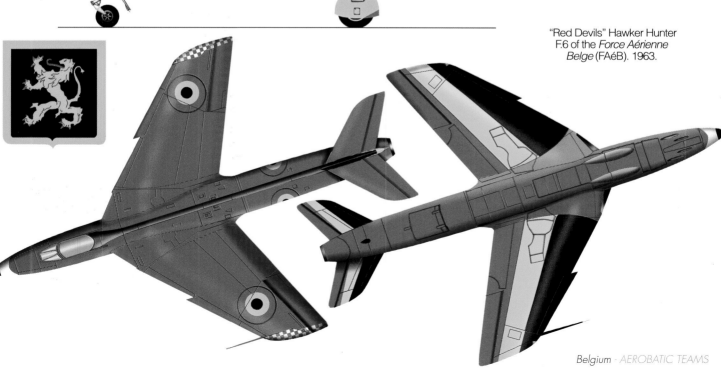

"Red Devils" Hawker Hunter F.6 of the *Force Aérienne Belge* (FAéB). 1963.

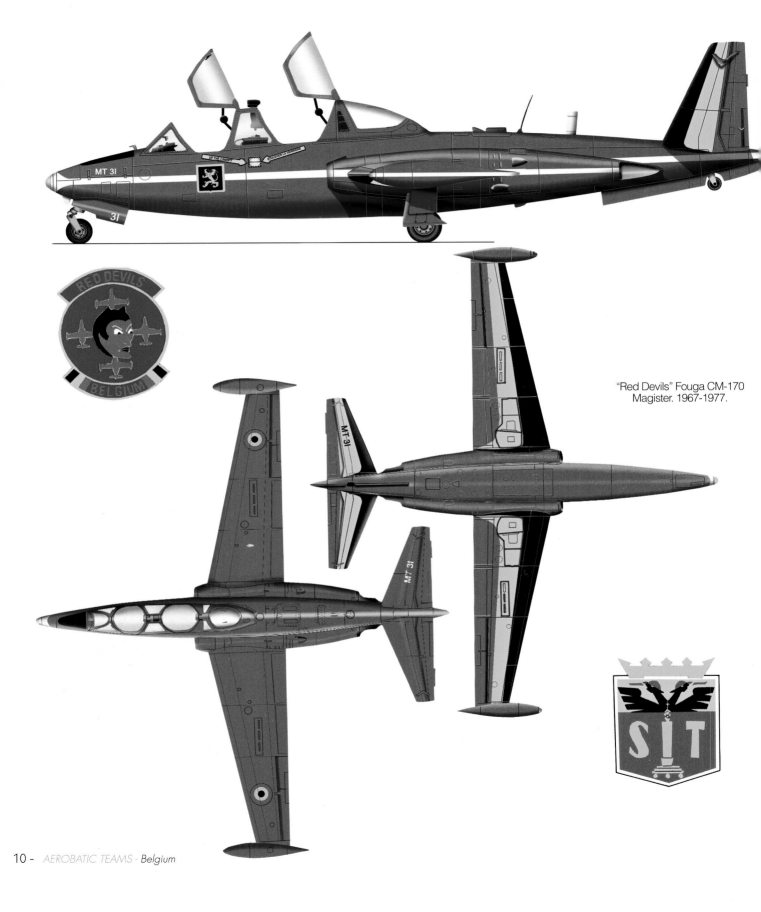

"Red Devils" Fouga CM-170
Magister. 1967-1977.

BRAZIL
"Esquadrilha da Fumaça"

Created in 1952 by the flying instructors of the Brazilian air academy, the "Esquadrilha da Fumaça" display team (smoke squadron, a name given due to the aircraft being equipped with smoke generators) flew with the North American T-6 until 1968, the year in which these aircraft were replaced with the Fouga Magister (locally designated T-24). The planes were painted in the colours of the Brazilian flag, these being green, yellow and blue. Due to the weather conditions in the country and the oil crisis at the beginning of the nineteen-seventies, the display team was forced to replace its Fouga Magisters after a little more than forty displays, and went back to flying its venerable T-6 aircraft.

Disbanded in 1977 due to financial problems, the Esquadrilha da Fumaça was reformed in 1982 and equipped with the Brazilian made single engine Embraer EMB-312 (T-27) Tucano. These were initially painted like all Brazilian training aircraft in red and white, then, in 2002, in the green, yellow and blue of the national flag.

Today, the Esquadrilha da Fumaça flies with the Embraer T27 Tucano.

(Photo Coll. G. Paloque)

Fouga CM-170 Magister of
the *Força Aerea Brasileira*
(Brazilian Air Force)
"Esquadrilha da Fumaça",
1969.

CANADA

"The Blue Devils"

The "Blue Devils" display team was created in 1949 as part of No 410 Squadron based at St Hubert, Longueuil, Quebec.

This was the RCAF's (Royal Canadian Air Force) first display team and was equipped with six De Havilland Vampires, undertaking displays in Canada as well as the USA. One of its pilots was killed on 25 July 1946 whilst training near St Hubert. The display team was disbanded at the end of 1951 and the Vampires decommissioned within the RCAF.

seasons. A support Lockheed T-33, with the same livery as the Sabres, followed the display team wherever it went.

"The Golden Centennaires"

The "Golden Centennaires" display team was formed in 1967 during Canada's centenary. celebrations. With its Canadair CT-114 Tutor, it took part in one hundred air shows in Canada and eight others in the USA. It was disbanded following a final display at the Montreal World's Fair at the end of 1967.

De Havilland DH 100 Vampire Mk 5 of No 410 Squadron, Royal Canadian Air Force (RCAF). "Blue Devils" aerobatic display team, 1949.

"Sky Lancers"

A display team equipped with North American F-86 Sabres, named the "Sky Lancers" was created within the 2nd Wing during the 1955 season, where it carried out twenty displays. A year later, it was the 4th Wing based at Baden-Soellingen, in Germany, that was given the responsibility of the team, keeping the same pilots and name. However, on 2 March 1956, four of the five "Sky Lancers" pilots were killed during a training flight south-east of Strasbourg in the Vosges. This brought an end to the RCAF's display teams for several years.

"The Golden Hawks"

To celebrate the RCAF's 35th anniversary and the 50 years of Canadian military aviation, a display team comprising of six Canadair Sabre Mk.5 named the "Golden Hawks" was created in 1959. The planes were given a golden livery with a large stylised red and white hawk on each side of the fuselage. The display team continued giving displays until February 1964 when it was disbanded for budgetary reasons. It had carried out 317 displays throughout its five

"The Snowbirds"

The "Snowbirds" were created in 1971 by Colonel O. B. Philip, the leader of the "Golden Centennaires". They carried out their first display with their seven Canadair CT-114 Tutors, in July the same year at the Moose Jaw air show in the province of Saskatchewan. They then flew at large air shows all over Canada. Two solo planes were added to the display team in 1972, a year in which they undertook twenty-five displays.

It was not until 1974 that the "Snowbirds" were authorised to carry out aerobatics in formation and they adopted a red and white livery for their aircraft, something which is still in use today. They flew at eighty air shows in the 1974 season.

The Snowbirds undertook an unusual display on 11 May 1975 at Inuvik (North West Territories) when they flew at midnight.

The display team became permanent in 1977 under the name of Canadian Forces Air Demonstration Team the, on 1 April 1978, the "Snowbirds" were given squadron status and renamed the 431st Air Demonstration Squadron. On

(Photos CAF)

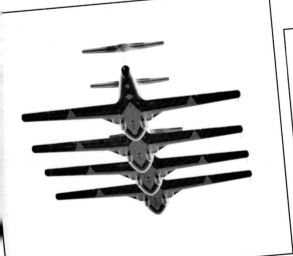

Canadair Sabre Mk 5 of the «Sky Lancers» of the RCAF. 1955.

"Sky Lancers" Canadair Sabre Mk 6 during their stay at Baden (Federal Republic of Germany), in 1956.

this year, there was a serious accident during a display at Grande Prairie (Alberta) when a pilot was forced to eject following the failure of his flight control surfaces. The pilot did not survive.

Eight years later, the display team flew at the opening and closing ceremony of Expo 86 in Vancouver. The "Snowbirds" also flew during the opening ceremony of the Winter Olympics at Calgary in 1988. On 3 September 1989, two planes collided in mid-air during a display at Toronto; one of the planes crashed into Lake Ontario, killing its pilot, whilst the other pilot managed to safely eject.

In 1990, the display team celebrated its twentieth anniversary and also carried out its one thousandth display. In the autumn of the following year, it took part in Disneyworld's twentieth anniversary.

In 1993, the "Snowbirds" began flying in displays outside of the North-American continent, participating in three air shows at Guadalajara in Mexico. In the same year, the display team led by Major Dean Rainkie, formed a one-off formation with a Su-27 of the "Russian Vityaz" at an air show held at Abbotsford, in British Columbia.

A similar event took place at the same place in 1995, when Major Steve Hill flew alongside the Northern Lights, at Halcones and with the Esquadrilha da Fumaça.

In 1999, the "Snowbirds" received the Queen's Colours, representing their twenty-five years of service.

One of this aerobatic display team's particularities was that it was the only one in the world not to have a support aircraft. As a totally autonomous unit, it used its own Tutors to transport personnel and equipment. There were replacement aircraft in the case any technical problems.

"Red Knights"

Originally, "Red Knight" was the name of the sole Canadian Canadair CT-33 Silver Star, painted red and which flew in North America between 1958 and 1969. The plane flew before the displays carried out by other Canadian display teams such as the "Golden Hawks" and, later, the "Golden Centennaires".

Seventeen pilots flew this plane during the course of its career with the Royal Canadian Air Force, with a second plane having joined it for a short period. These

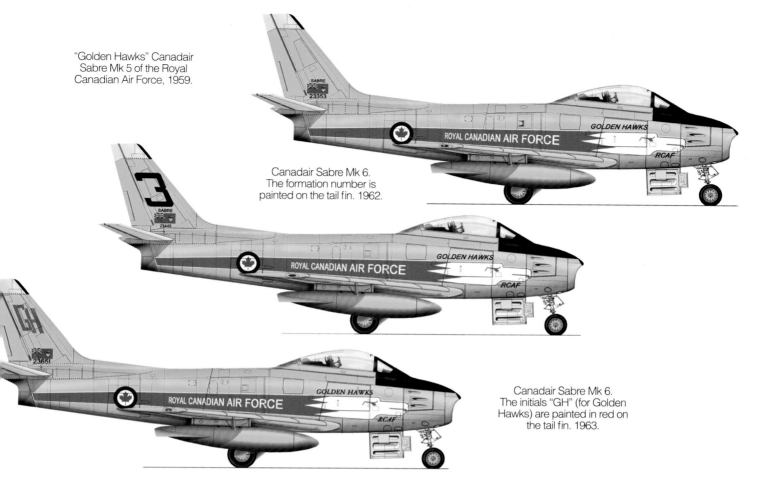

"Golden Hawks" Canadair Sabre Mk 5 of the Royal Canadian Air Force, 1959.

Canadair Sabre Mk 6. The formation number is painted on the tail fin. 1962.

Canadair Sabre Mk 6. The initials "GH" (for Golden Hawks) are painted in red on the tail fin. 1963.

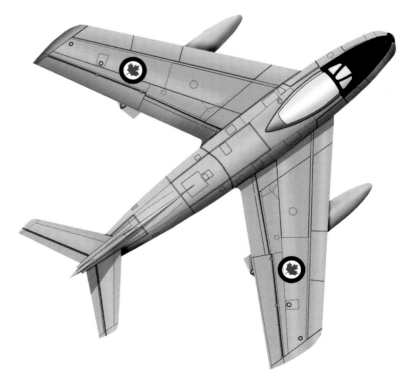

two-plane displays did not last for long and came to an end with the accident which happened on 21 August 1963. During the RCAF Day at Gimli, the two planes were carrying out an aerobatic manoeuvre when one of the pilots, Wayne MacLellan, realised that he was flying too low and decided to break off the manoeuvre. Unfortunately, the second pilot did not understand what MacLellan was doing and crashed into the ground, killing himself.

During the 1968-1969 season, two "Golden Centenaires" Tutors were repainted in "Red Knight" colours to replace the T-33. 21 May 1968 saw another accident during a photo session, with a plane crashing and the death of its pilot. Sadly, this tragic incident was followed by another on 13 July 1969, when the "Red Knight" suffered an engine failure and crashed whilst attempting an emergency landing, killing its pilot. This series of crashes led the RCAF to seriously reconsider its program. However, the lack of experienced pilots meant that the "Red Knight" program came to a definitive end.

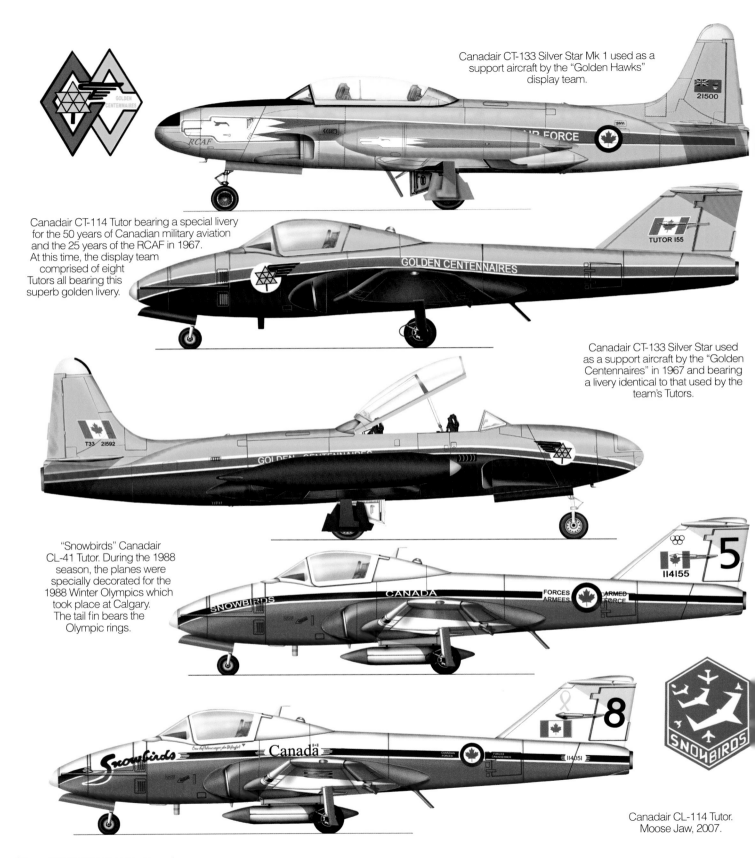

Canadair CT-133 Silver Star Mk 1 used as a support aircraft by the "Golden Hawks" display team.

Canadair CT-114 Tutor bearing a special livery for the 50 years of Canadian military aviation and the 25 years of the RCAF in 1967. At this time, the display team comprised of eight Tutors all bearing this superb golden livery.

Canadair CT-133 Silver Star used as a support aircraft by the "Golden Centennaires" in 1967 and bearing a livery identical to that used by the team's Tutors.

"Snowbirds" Canadair CL-41 Tutor. During the 1988 season, the planes were specially decorated for the 1988 Winter Olympics which took place at Calgary. The tail fin bears the Olympic rings.

Canadair CL-114 Tutor. Moose Jaw, 2007.

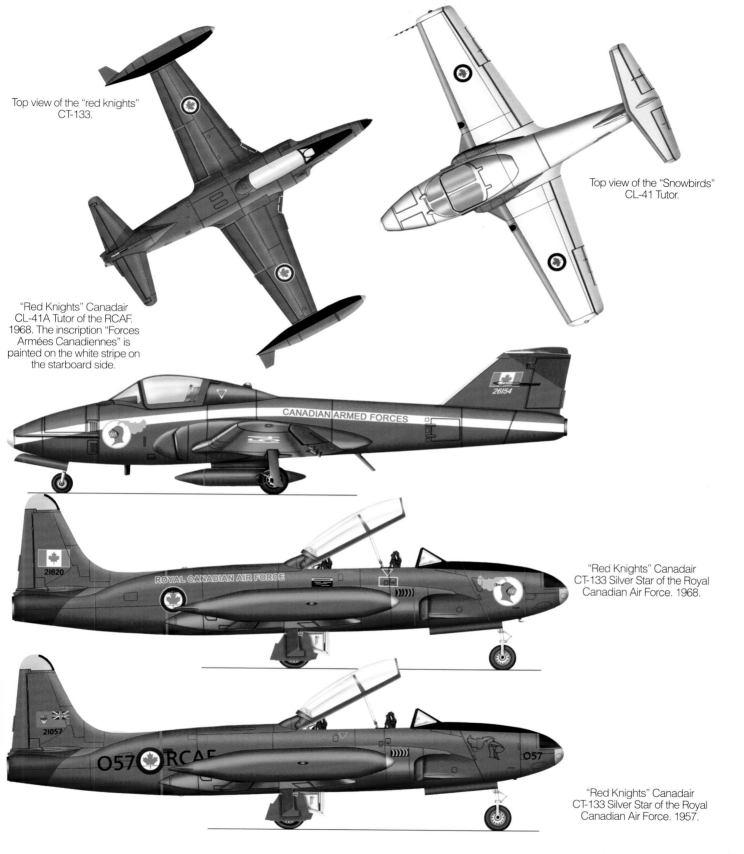

Top view of the "red knights" CT-133.

Top view of the "Snowbirds" CL-41 Tutor.

"Red Knights" Canadair CL-41A Tutor of the RCAF. 1968. The inscription "Forces Armées Canadiennes" is painted on the white stripe on the starboard side.

CANADIAN ARMED FORCES

26154

"Red Knights" Canadair CT-133 Silver Star of the Royal Canadian Air Force. 1968.

21620

ROYAL CANADIAN AIR FORCE

21057

O57 RCAF

O57

"Red Knights" Canadair CT-133 Silver Star of the Royal Canadian Air Force. 1957.

MONGOLIA

C H I N A

TIBET

BANGLADESH

INDIA   MYANMAR

CHINA

"August 1st"

The *Zhÿngguó Rénmín Jiûfàngjün Kÿngjün*, People's Liberation Army Air Force aerobatic display team, was created on 12 February 1962. At the beginning, it comprised of nine JJ-5, a Chinese made aircraft derived from the Soviet two-seater MiG-15UTI and MiG-17U.

In 1997, the display team was named "Ba Yi" ("August 1st", the day of the Chinese People's Republic air force was created, and equipped with six Chengdu J-7EB P, the Chinese version of the MiG-21, with five other reserve aircraft. Its first display under its new name took place on 20 December 1997 at its home base at Yangcun. At the time, the planes were painted white and

red and bore red numbers at the front from between 01 and 11.

In June 1997, three pilots were killed during a training flight over their base. The three planes collided whilst carrying out a loop in a row. In 1998, another aircraft crashed near the airport of Chongming, near Zhulaï.

In 2001, the display team was officially designated as the 81st Squadron (aerobatic) of the 70th air regiment, changing the livery of its new J-7GB aircraft which were painted white and light blue.

During the 2008 Olympic Games, the display team flew with five Chengdu J-7GB, each one bearing one of the colours of the Olympic rings. In May 2009, the display team received the Chengdu J-10.

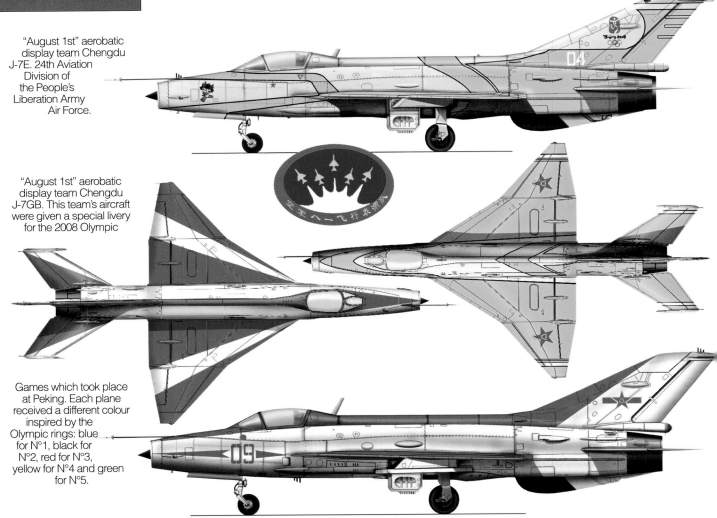

"August 1st" aerobatic display team Chengdu J-7E. 24th Aviation Division of the People's Liberation Army Air Force.

"August 1st" aerobatic display team Chengdu J-7GB. This team's aircraft were given a special livery for the 2008 Olympic

Games which took place at Peking. Each plane received a different colour inspired by the Olympic rings: blue for N°1, black for N°2, red for N°3, yellow for N°4 and green for N°5.

CZECHOSLOVAKIA

In the mid nineteen-fifties, the Czechoslovakian air force *(Ceskoslovenske letectvo)* had a display team equipped with the MiG-15bis, each one bearing, in way of decoration, a red lightning flash painted on the fuselage and which continued on the wings.

In 1954, a MiG-15, code "EP-02", carried out solo displays.

This aircraft was entirely painted in red on the upper part of the fuselage.

On 1 September 1957, the team, which had no name, took part in an air show at Cottbus, one hundred kilometres south of Berlin, at the time of the German Democratic Republic. its planes bore the following codes: 3213, 3233, 3234 and 3237.

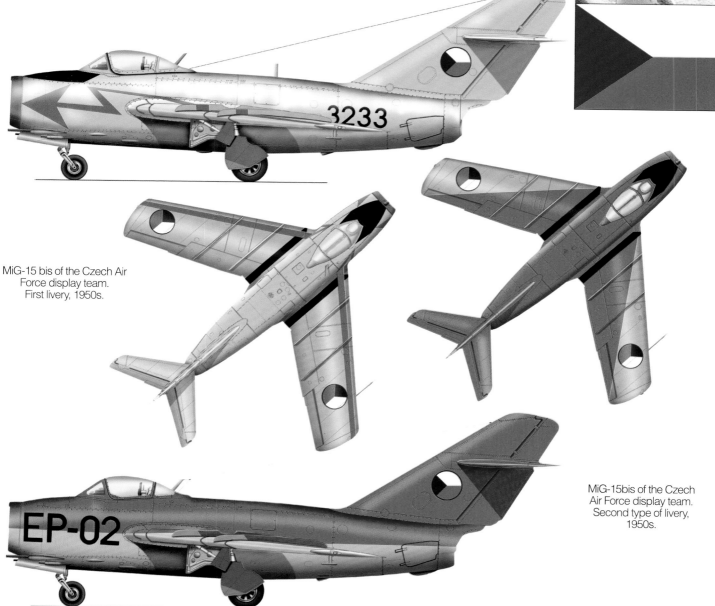

MiG-15 bis of the Czech Air Force display team. First livery, 1950s.

MiG-15bis of the Czech Air Force display team. Second type of livery, 1950s.

FRANCE

"Patrouille de France"

The Patrouille de France was created within the 3e Escadre de Chasse based at Reims in April 1953. At this time it was equipped with four Republic F-84G Thunderjets and placed under the command of Commandant Delachenal. Taking turns for the command of the display team, the 2e Escadre de Chasse de Dijon formed a team in 1954, equipped this time with four Dassault MD 450 Ouragan. The following year saw the turn of the 12e Escadre de Chasse based at Cambrai and the 4e Escadre of the Bremgarten air base (West Germany) in 1956.

In order to continue the rotation of squadrons and with the aim of promoting French aeronautical technology, the French Air Force's general staff decided to create a second display team within the 12e Escadre at Cambrai, equipped this time with the Dassault Mystère IVA. This team was given the task of carrying out overseas displays, whilst the 4e Escadre equipped with the Ouragan flew at home. Important changes were made in 1957, when the Patrouille de France made its home for several years at the Dijon air base as part of the 2e Escadre de Chasse, also equipped with the Mystère IVA.

In 1960, the Patrouille de France went from four to twelve aircraft and two years later, was based at Nancy with the 7e Escadre de Chasse, as the 2e Escadre at Dijon had begun to receive the brand new Mirage IIIC.

Due to budget cuts in 1964, the display team was disbanded. However, as the "Patrouille de l'École de l'Air" had existed since 1957 at Salon-de-Provence, flying the cheap but nimble Fouga CM 170R Magister, the general staff decided that the Patrouille de l'École de l'Air would take up the name of "Patrouille de France" and was made up of six Fouga aircraft.

On 4 June 1967, Capitaine Didier Duthois crashed during a display at the Bourget air show and was killed.

In 1971, the Patrouille de France adopted a new "bleu de France" livery for its planes and comprised of eleven Magisters in 1972. The team celebrated its 25th anniversary in July 1978 and two years later, in 1980, at the end of the air show season, the Fougas were replaced with Alpha Jets. 1980 was also a dark year for the Patrouille as two of its Fougas collided whilst carrying out an inverted synchronised manoeuvre, killing the two pilots.

In 1981, the team had seven Alpha Jets, increasing to eight the following year. The Patrouille de France lost its first Alpha Jet in 1981, during a training flight north of Aix-en-Provence and by 2009, the team had lost eleven planes in accidents with four pilots killed.

Republic F-84G Thunderjet, of the Escadron de Chasse 1/3 "Navarre". Reims, 1953.

Dassault MD 450 Ouragan n° 420 (12e Escadre de Chasse). Cambrai, 1955.

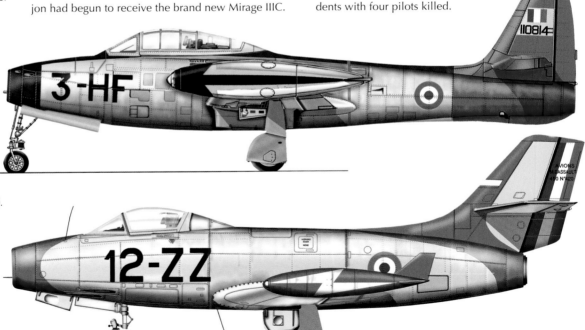

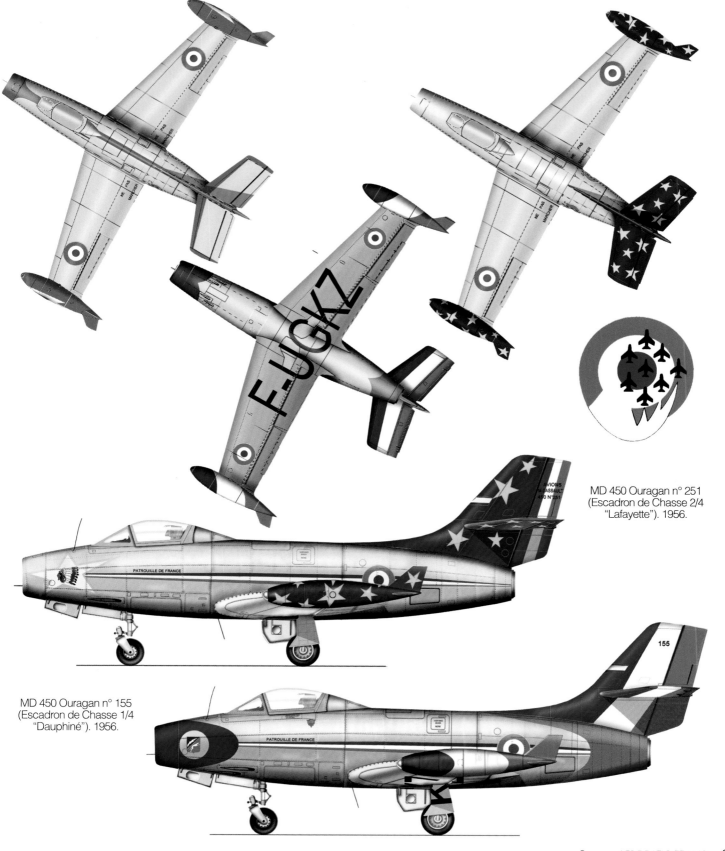

MD 450 Ouragan n° 251
(Escadron de Chasse 2/4
"Lafayette"). 1956.

MD 450 Ouragan n° 155
(Escadron de Chasse 1/4
"Dauphiné"). 1956.

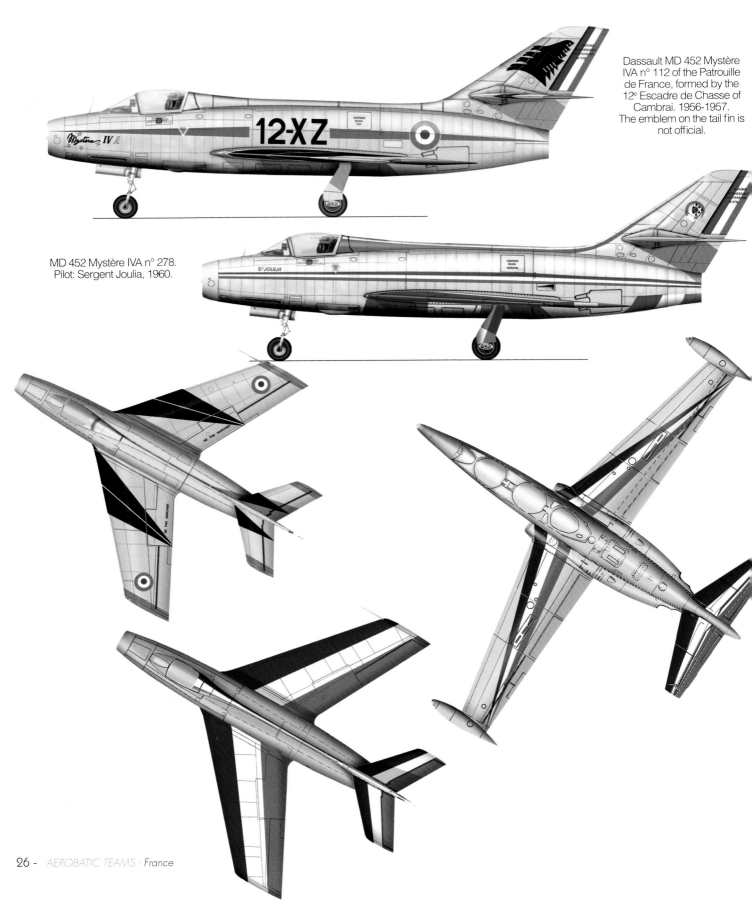

Dassault MD 452 Mystère IVA n° 112 of the Patrouille de France, formed by the 12e Escadre de Chasse of Cambrai. 1956-1957. The emblem on the tail fin is not official.

MD 452 Mystère IVA n° 278. Pilot: Sergent Joulia, 1960.

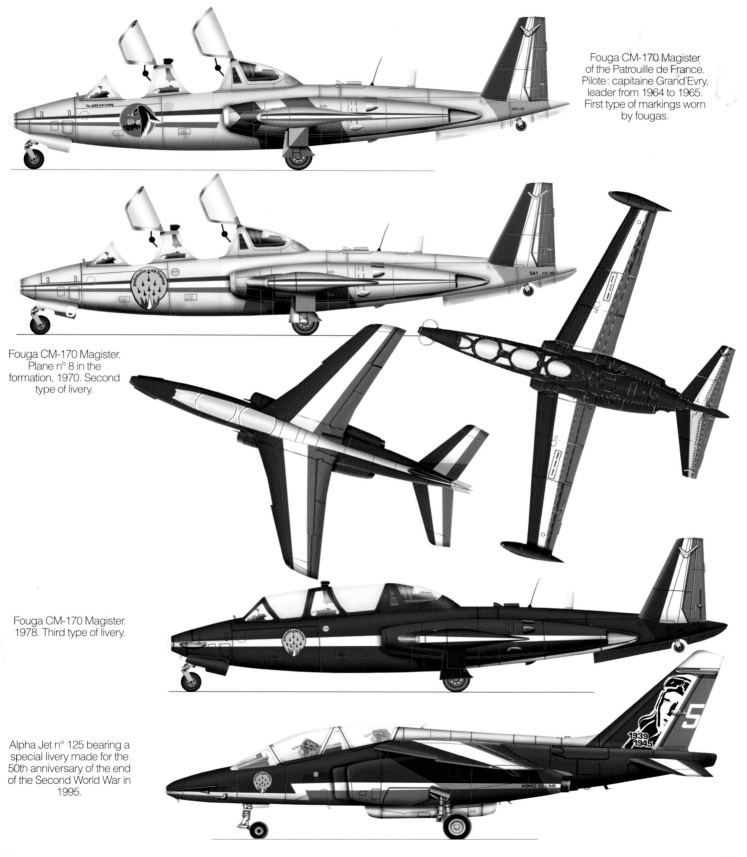

Fouga CM-170 Magister
of the Patrouille de France.
Pilote : capitaine Grand'Evry,
leader from 1964 to 1965.
First type of markings worn
by fougas.

Fouga CM-170 Magister.
Plane n° 8 in the
formation, 1970. Second
type of livery.

Fouga CM-170 Magister.
1978. Third type of livery.

Alpha Jet n° 125 bearing a
special livery made for the
50th anniversary of the end
of the Second World War in
1995.

GREECE

"Hellenic Flame"

The "Hellenic Flame" aerobatic display team was formed in August 1957 within the 341 Mira (squadron) of the *Elliniki Polemiki Aeroporia* (Greek Air Force) based at Tanagra and began training with five Canadair Sabre Mk.2, a number that was then increased to seven aircraft. Following numerous displays in Western Europe and Turkey, the team was disbanded in September 1964.

North American F-86E Sabre of the *Elliniki Polemiki Aeroporia* (Greek Air Force), 1963.

INDIA

"The Thunderbolts"

India's first display team was formed for the Indian air Force's (Bharatiya Vayu Sena) Golden Jubilee in 1982. Named "The Thunderbolts", they flew with nine Hawker Hunter F.56A supplied by No 20 Squadron. The team gave their last display with the Hunter in 1989, and the planes were retired from service the following year. They were replaced the same year with four Indian built HAL HJT-16 Kiran Mk. II training aircraft.

"Thunderbolts" Hawker Hunter Mk.56 of the Indian Air Force, 1982.

"Surya Kiran"

On 27 May 1996, two Kiran Mk. II plus a replacement aircraft, were added to "The Thunderbolts" and the display team changed its name for the one it currently uses "Surya Kiran" (sun rays). It carried out its first display on 8 October 1996 during the *Bharatiya Vayu Sena Day* (Indian Air Force), at Palam. The following year, the team numbered nine aircraft and two solos.

The "Surya Kiran" flew abroad for the first time in 2001 at the Sri Lankan capital Colombo.

A serious accident happened on 18 March 2006 during a formation training flight with three aircraft at the Bidar (Karnataka) air base. One of the team's planes collided with a wingman at low altitude and crashed into the ground, killing both pilots.

22 December 2007 saw another of the team's aircraft crash whilst taking off from the Bhubaneswar air base, however, this time the pilot escaped unharmed.

On 21 January 2009, two of the team's Kirans collided during a training flight, one pilot was killed and the other seriously injured.

The display team today has nine Kiran Mk. II (plus two replacement aircraft), 13 pilots and fifty ground crew. The "Surya Kiran" are based at Bidar and undertake thirty displays every year.

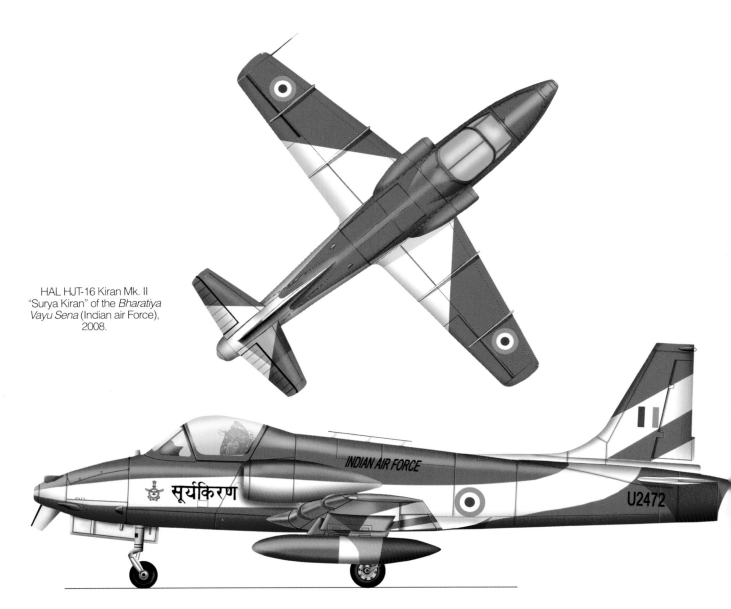

HAL HJT-16 Kiran Mk. II "Surya Kiran" of the *Bharatiya Vayu Sena* (Indian air Force), 2008.

IRAN

"The Golden Crown"

In the mid nineteen-fifties, a detachment of pilots of the *Rasmieh Niruyeh havaieh Shahanshahieh Iran* (Imperial Iranian Air Force/IIAF) began training at the USAFE base (US Air Force Europe) at Fürstenfeldbruck, West Germany, with the Republic F-84G Thunderjet, a jet that had recently been purchased by Iran. One of the pilots, Captain Nader Jahanbani, had seen the "Skyblazers" in action and decided to form a display team within the IIAF. When the detachment returned to Iran, he formed a display team comprising of four F-84G Thunderjets which adopted, in June 1958, the official name of "Imperial Iranian Air Force Golden Crown Acrojet Team".

The same year saw an accident during a display, killing a pilot. The following year, the team had nine Thunderjets, a number reduced to six in 1960.

Beginning in 1961, the "Golden Crown" began flying with six F-86F Sabres and in 1963, during a training flight, two of these planes collided and crashed, killing the pilots. The team, therefore, ended the year with only four planes.

In 1964, the "Golden Crown" began flying in a formation of five planes and, two years later, one of its pilots had to eject due to a bird strike, but escaped unharmed.

Five Northrop F-5A Freedom Fighters were delivered to the team in 1968, but the following year, it had to fly once more with six Sabres. The same year saw a crash during a display, resulting in the death of a pilot.

In 1970, the "Golden Crown" reverted back to a five plane formation, flying for the last year with the F-86F Sabre.

The following year the team briefly got back its six F-5A. Another accident, in which a pilot was killed, reduced the formation to five aircraft for the rest of the season.

The US Navy "Blue Angels" took part in an air show at Tehran in 1973, accompanied by the six F-5A of the "Golden Crown". The following year saw another accident and the death of a pilot. In 1976, the "Golden Crown" received seven F-5E Tiger II aircraft, increasing to eight planes during the last two years of the team's existence. The team was disbanded following the Islamic Revolution in 1979.

"Golden Crown", Republic F-84G Thunderjet, the aerobatic display team of the *Rasmieh Niruyeh havaieh Shahanshahieh Iran* (Imperial Iranian Air Force), 1958.

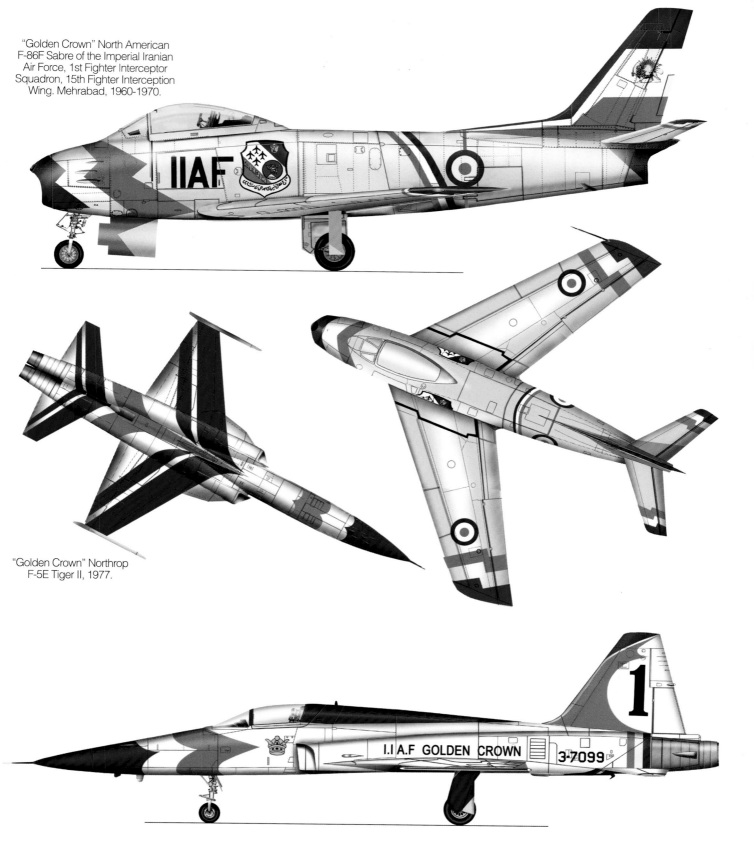

"Golden Crown" North American
F-86F Sabre of the Imperial Iranian
Air Force, 1st Fighter Interceptor
Squadron, 15th Fighter Interception
Wing. Mehrabad, 1960-1970.

"Golden Crown" Northrop
F-5E Tiger II, 1977.

I.I A.F GOLDEN CROWN   3-7099

ISRAEL

IAF aerobatic Team

Starting in 1960, the Fouga Magister CM-170 (locally named" Tzukit") replaced the T-6 of the *Heyl Ha'Avir* (Israeli Air Force) flying school. As soon as they were put into service, a display team was formed at the Hatzerim air base with the school's flight instructors. This team flew displays during the passing out ceremonies at the school, as well as the country's independence ceremonies, but did not take part in any other displays outside of Israel. The team does not have an official name and only flies a few displays per year.

Fouga CM-170 Magister of the *Heyl Ha'Avir* (Israeli Air Force), 1967.

ITALY

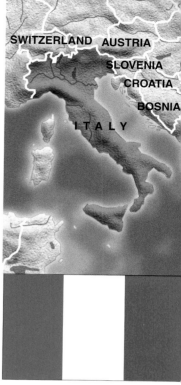

"Getti Tonanti"

The "Getti Tonanti" (Thunder Jets) were formed in 1953, within the 5° Stormo based at Villafranca di Verona, in Venetia and flew with the Republic F-84G Thunderjet until 1955. It was reformed in 1959 at the Rimini air base (Emilia-Romagna), attached this time to the 5a Aerobrigata and equipped with the Republic F-84F Thunderstreak. This display team flew at the opening ceremony of the Rome Olympic Games in 1960, with each plane painted in one of the colours of the Olympic rings.

The "Getti Tonanti" were disbanded at the end of the same year.

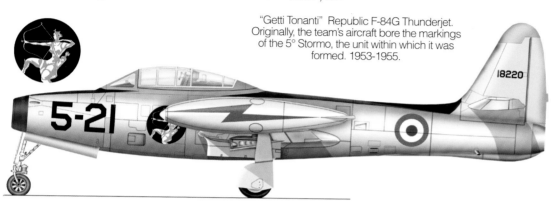

"Getti Tonanti" Republic F-84G Thunderjet. Originally, the team's aircraft bore the markings of the 5° Stormo, the unit within which it was formed. 1953-1955.

"Getti Tonanti" Republic F-84F Thunderstreak. Pilot: Sergente Maggiore (sergeant-major) Gregorio Baschrotto. 1959-1960.
Each of the teams planes had an individual colour: orange (F-84 MM — Matricole Militare — 5-36591), yellow (MM 5-785), black (MM 5-648), red (MM 5-653), green 5-619 green and white for MM 7-721, the replacement aircraft. In 1960, the Olympic Rings were added to the tail fin for the summer Olympics that took place in Rome. These rings were white on the red and black planes, and white for the others.

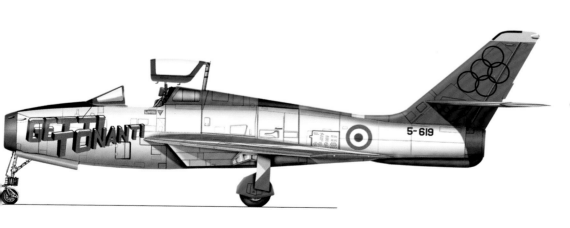

"Getti Tonanti" Republic F-84F Thunderstreak. Pilot: Tenente (lieutenant) Mauro Ciceroni, 1960.

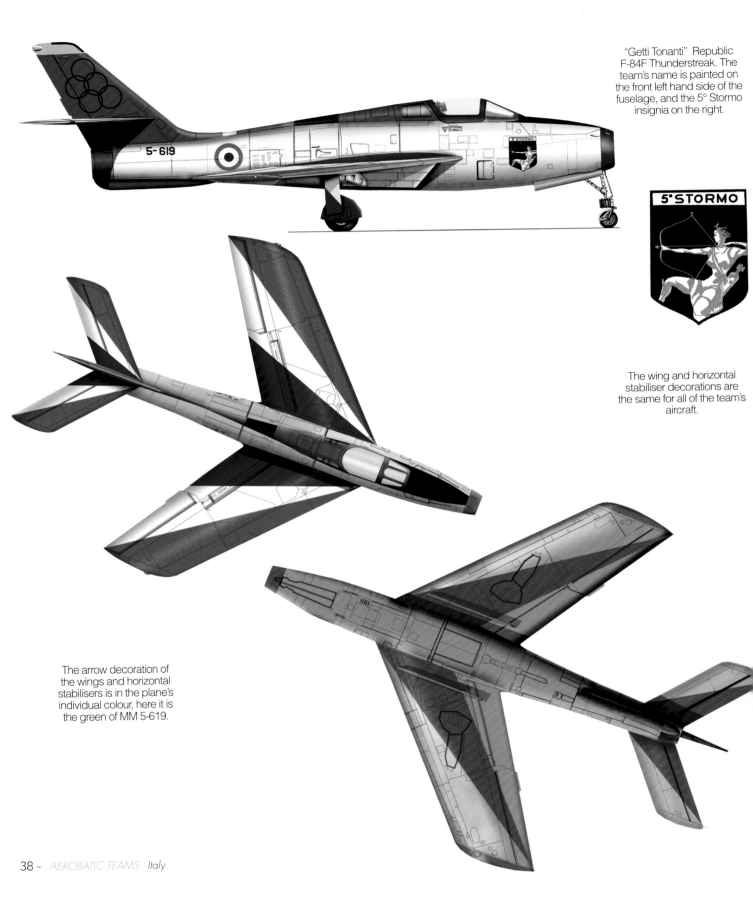

"Getti Tonanti" Republic F-84F Thunderstreak. The team's name is painted on the front left hand side of the fuselage, and the 5° Stormo insignia on the right.

5-619

5° STORMO

The wing and horizontal stabiliser decorations are the same for all of the team's aircraft.

The arrow decoration of the wings and horizontal stabilisers is in the plane's individual colour, here it is the green of MM 5-619.

"Cavallino Rampante"

This display team was formed in 1950, within the 4a Aerobrigata (air brigade) at the Grosseto air base, Tuscany, and flew until 1952, the year in which it was disbanded. It was equipped with the De Havilland Vampire Mk.5 which had no special livery.

In 1956, still at Grosseto, the team was reformed under the name of "Cavallino Rampante" (rampant horse), but this time equipped with the Canadair Sabre Mk.4 (a version of the F-86 made under licence in Canada). Its career ended in 1957.

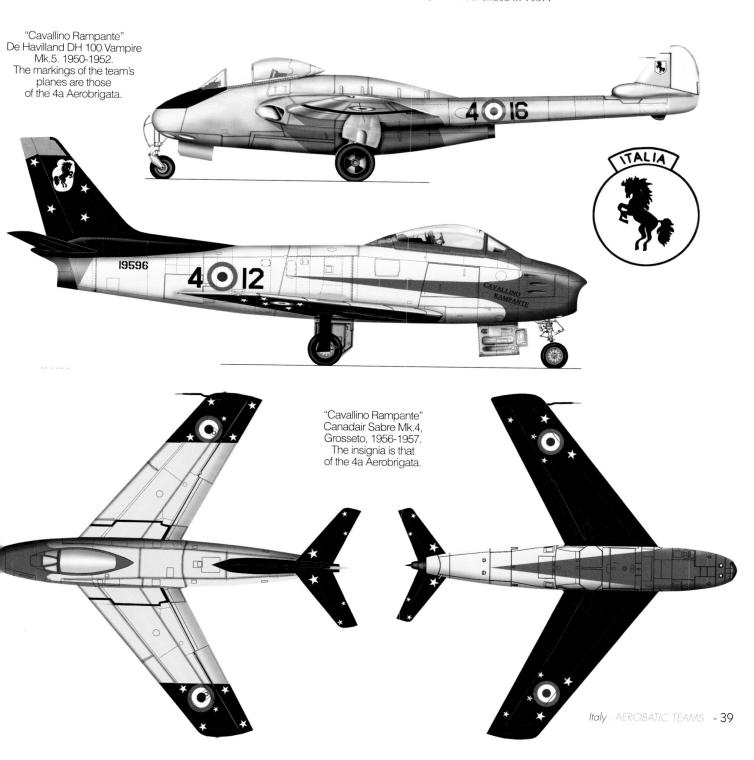

"Cavallino Rampante"
De Havilland DH 100 Vampire
Mk.5. 1950-1952.
The markings of the team's
planes are those
of the 4a Aerobrigata.

"Cavallino Rampante"
Canadair Sabre Mk.4,
Grosseto, 1956-1957.
The insignia is that
of the 4a Aerobrigata.

"Tigri Bianche"

The "Tigri Bianche" (White Tigers) flew with the F-84G Thunderjet between 1955-1956. They were part of the 51a Aerobrigata based at Istran, Venetia. This was the first display team of the *Aeronautica Militare Italiana* (AMI/Italian Air Force) to go to Canada and the USA.

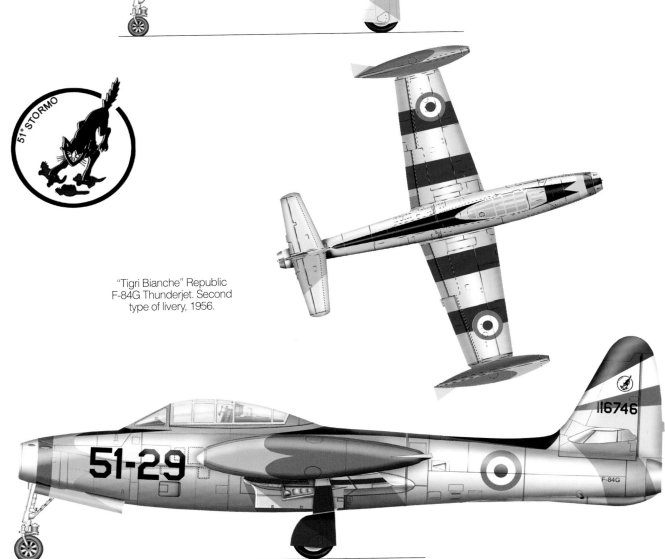

"Tigri Bianche" Republic
F-84G Thunderjet, Istrana,
1955.
First type of livery. The tail
fin insignia is that of the 51°
Stormo.

"Tigri Bianche" Republic
F-84G Thunderjet. Second
type of livery, 1956.

"Diavoli Rossi"

During its existence between 1957 and 1959, the "Diavoli Rossi" (Red Devils) was based at Ghedi, in Lombardy, and attached to the 6a Aerobrigata, equipped with the F-84F Thunderstreak. The "Red Devils" flew their first display on 10 March 1958 at Bitburg, West Germany, and their last on 17 May the following year at New York.
The team was awarded with the title of the best NATO aerobatic display team, during a display at Ypenburg, Holland.

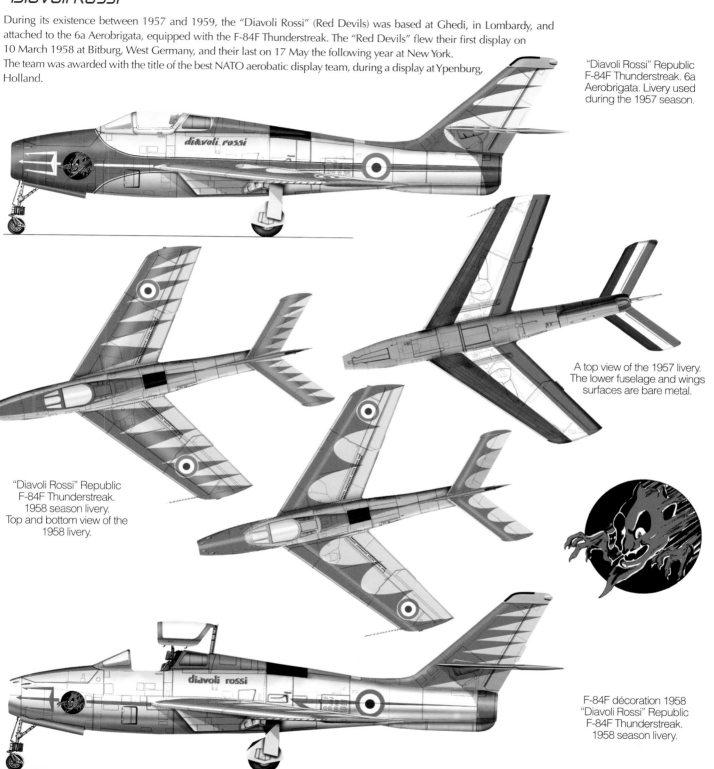

"Diavoli Rossi" Republic F-84F Thunderstreak. 6a Aerobrigata. Livery used during the 1957 season.

A top view of the 1957 livery. The lower fuselage and wings surfaces are bare metal.

"Diavoli Rossi" Republic F-84F Thunderstreak. 1958 season livery. Top and bottom view of the 1958 livery.

F-84F décoration 1958 "Diavoli Rossi" Republic F-84F Thunderstreak. 1958 season livery.

Insigne of the 2a Aerobrigata

"Lanceri Neri"

The "Lanceri Neri" (Black Lancers) display team was formed at the Cameri air base (Piedmont) in 1958, within the 2a Aerobrigata. It flew with the Canadair Sabre Mk.4 (F-86E) and was disbanded in 1959.

"Lanceri Neri" display team Canadair Sabre Mk.4. 2°Aerobrigata. 1958-1959.

Top and bottom view of the "Lanceri Neri" Sabre.

"Frecce Tricolori"

The 313° Gruppo Addestramento Aerobatico, a squadron solely dedicated to aerobatic displays, was created in 1961 at the Rivolto airbase in the region of Frioul and given the official name of Frecce Tricolori (Tricolour Arrows). Equipped with the F-86E from 1961 to 1963, it then flew with the Fiat G-91 from 1964 to 1981, the year in which it switched to the Aermacchi MB-339A.

On 28 August 1988 at the Ramstein air show near Frankfurt, the solo plane of the Frecce Tricolori collided with two other planes that crashed onto the runway, whilst the solo plane hit spectators. Seventy people lost their lives, including the three pilots from the display team.

On 27 October 2002, one of the team's MB-339 aircraft was the victim of a bird strike when landing at Rivolto, but the two pilots were able to eject safely.

Top and bottom view of the "Lanceri Neri" Sabres, the lower surfaces of the wings and horizontal stabilisers are tri-colour, whereas the upper surfaces are all black.

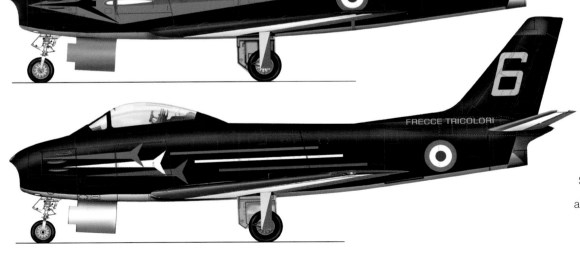

Frecce Tricolori Canadair Sabre Mk 4 bearing the last livery used by this type of aircraft. In 1962, the individual letter was replaced with a number. 1962-1964.

"Frecce Tricolori" Fiat G-91 PAN. The display team flew between 1954 and 1981 with this variant of the famous fighter, made from pre-production aircraft.

Macchi MB-339A. Definitive livery still in use in 2009.

JAPAN

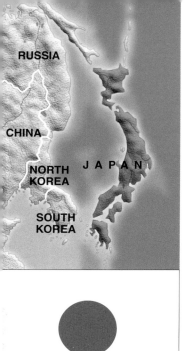

"The Blue Impulse"

The first Japanese display team was formed at Hamamatsuin 1958, equipped with the F-86F Sabre. This team was disbanded after only four displays.

Following a visit of the USAF "Thunderbirds" in 1959 with their F-100 Super Sabres, the command of the Japanese Air Defence Force decided to create an official display team, which was formed the following year, one again at Hamamatsu, and equipped with five F-86F Sabres. The new display team was named "Tenryu" and carried out its first display in on 4 March 1960 at Hamamatsu, but was quickly renamed "Blue Impulse" (translated literally in Japanese by Buru Inparusu). In 1961, the five Sabres received a blue and white livery, with the leader's plane painted in white and gold.

The team had its first accident on 21 July 1961 when an F-86F crashed into the sea, killing its pilot. In 1964, the "Blue Impulse" flew at the opening ceremony of the Olympic Games at Tokyo, using their smoke generators to make the Olympic rings. On 24 November 1965, an F-86F crashed at the end of the runway and the pilot ejected. Another Sabre crashed on 4 November 1972, near the river Iruma, following a display, but once again the pilot was able to eject.

The "Blue Impulse" replaced their Sabres with six Mitsubishi T-2 in February 1982, after having carried out 545 displays with their F-86F. The first air show with the new planes took place on 25 June at their new home base of Matsushima.

During a display simulating a bombing run at an air show at Hamamatsu on 14 November 1982, plane n° 4 hit a building, killing the pilot as well as eleven people on the ground. This resulted in the team being stopped from flying displays for one year. Another accident happened during a training flight on 4 July 1991 over Pacific Ocean, when planes n° 2 et 4 collided, killing both pilots. Once again, displays were suspended for a year.

The team's last display with the T-2 took place in December 1995 after 175 displays. The team was then equipped with the Kawasaki T-4, carrying out their first display on 5 April 1996.

The "Blue Impulse" first flew overseas in 1997 at the Nellis air show in Nevada.

Two Kawasaki T-4, planes n° 5 et 6, crashed on 4 June 2000 during a training flight, killing three pilots. Today, the "Blue Impulse" are based at Matsushima and have seven Kawasaki T-4, six of which are used during displays. The team comprises eleven pilots and approximately thirty ground crew.

"Blue Impulse" aerobatic display team North American F-86F Sabre of the Nihon Koku Jietai (Japanese Air Defence Force). 1er Kokudan (squadron). Komaki, 1962. The leader's plane was the only one to have this gold livery.

(Photos Blue Impulse/JSDAF)

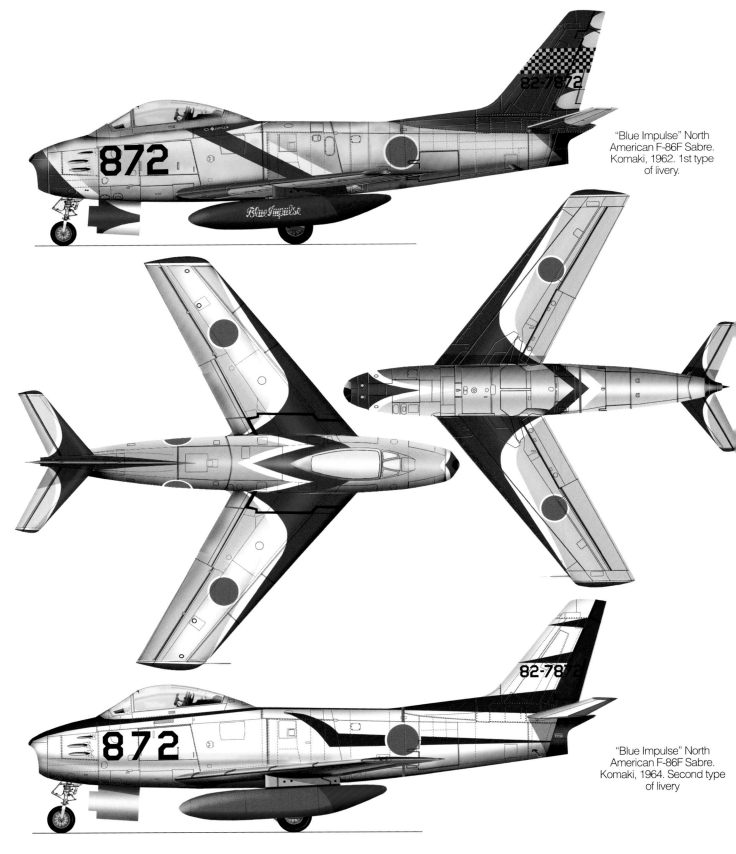

"Blue Impulse" North American F-86F Sabre. Komaki, 1962. 1st type of livery.

"Blue Impulse" North American F-86F Sabre. Komaki, 1964. Second type of livery

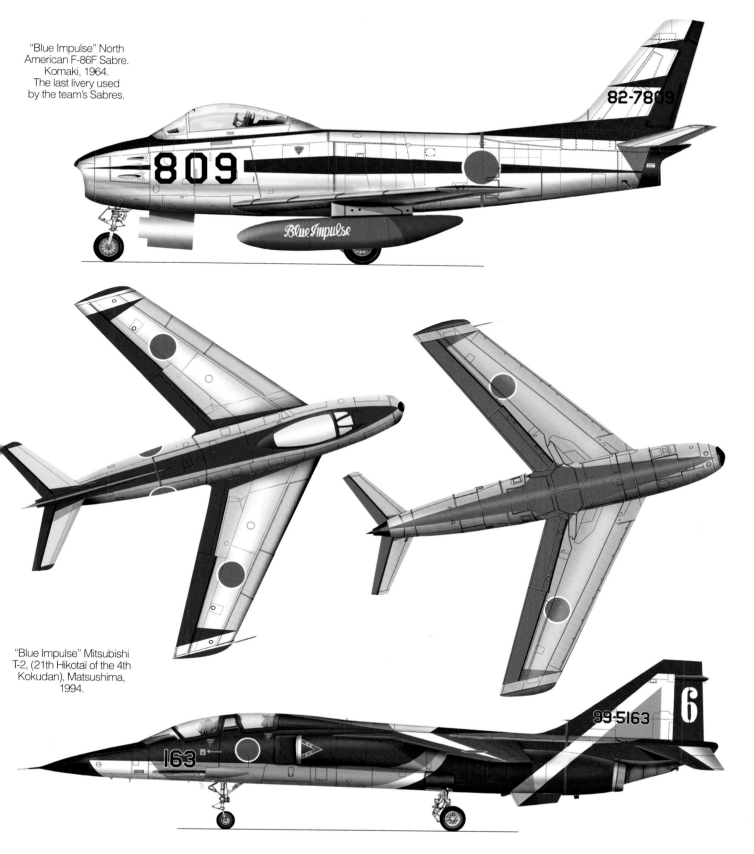

"Blue Impulse" North
American F-86F Sabre.
Komaki, 1964.
The last livery used
by the team's Sabres.

Blue Impulse

82-7809

809

"Blue Impulse" Mitsubishi
T-2, (21th Hikotaï of the 4th
Kokudan), Matsushima,
1994.

99-5163

163

6

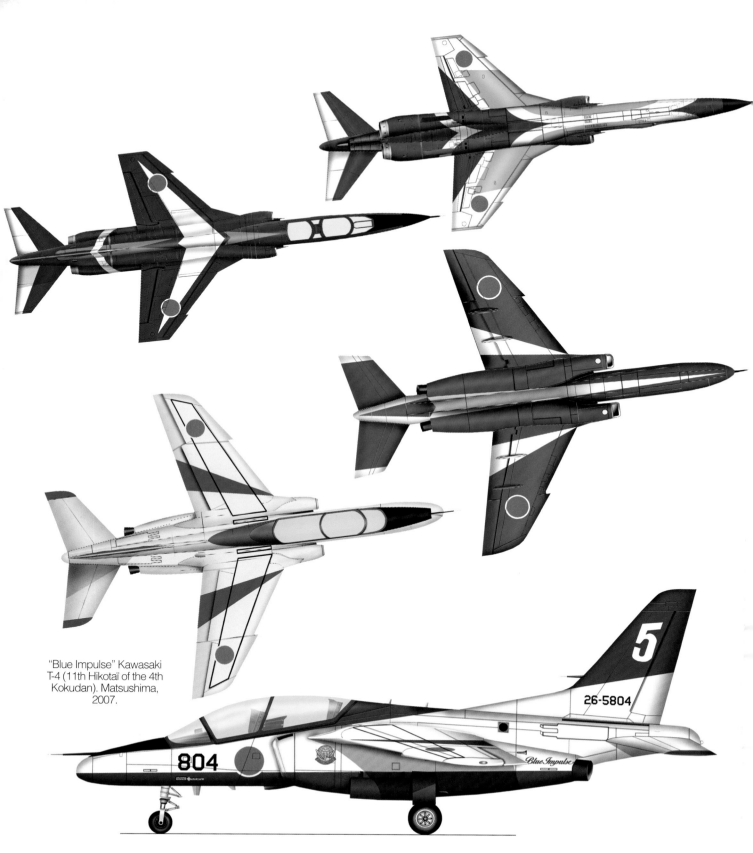

"Blue Impulse" Kawasaki
T-4 (11th Hikotaï of the 4th
Kokudan). Matsushima,
2007.

THE NETHERLANDS

"The Diamond Four"

At beginning of 1953, The *Koninklijke Luchtmacht* (The Royal Netherlands Air Force) decided to form an aerobatic display team named "Diamond Four" within No 327 Squadron based at Soesterberg and equipped with four Gloster Meteor Mk.8. This team flew displays all over Europe in 1953.

"The Gloster Meteor Mk.8"

A new display team, also equipped with four Meteor Mk.8 was created at the beginning of 1955, attached this time to No 323 Squadron. It carried out its first public outing on March 1955. One of the highlights of this team's short existence was the display it carried out at Sydenham, Ireland, in 1955. This air show was, in a way, the team's final bow.

"Dash Four"

The "Dash Four", equipped with F-84F aircraft, carried out its first display on 14 July 1956 at the Leeuwarden air base. On August of the same year, a competition took place at the Soesterberg air base and the "Dash Four", whose planes had been given a superb red, white and blue livery, finished second.

In 1957, the team took part in numerous displays at Dutch air bases and on 24 June 1958, one the national championships. The same year was the 45th anniversary of the KLu and on the following 5 July, a championship was organised for the Soesterberg air show, involving most of the NATO member nations (USA, Belgium, Denmark, UK, Greece, Portugal and Turkey). The "Dash Four" won this competition and were invited to fly at the World Congress of Flight at Las Vegas, organised between 12 - 19 April 1959. The team's pilots had to fly on USAF lent Thunderstreaks, but these planes were an older version than their own F-84F and they came across a few minor problems whilst training at the Luk air base.

On 9 April 1959, a short time before the air show, two Thunderstreaks collided. One of the pilots ejected, whilst the second managed to land his badly damaged plane. On 12 -15 April, the team carried out their display with USAF planes which were painted with orange stripes, the light blue emblem of the Dash Four and Dutch roundels. The team returned to Holland on 6 May and carried out its last display the following 19 June.

"Whiskey Four"

This display team was formed within No 314 Squadron and began flying with the F-84F in 1957, but just before its first display, it was disbanded following a training accident that resulted in the death of one of its pilots.
It was reformed in 1965 with the same name, equipped this time with four Lockheed T-33 bearing the standard markings of the "T-Birds" of the Koninklijke Luchtmacht on bare metal. On 8 June 1965, two pilots were killed when their planes collided during a display at the Woensdrecht air base. In 1966, the planes were given a specific green and white. The "Whiskey Four" were disbanded the following year.

NETHERLANDS

BELGIUM

GERMANY

FRANCE

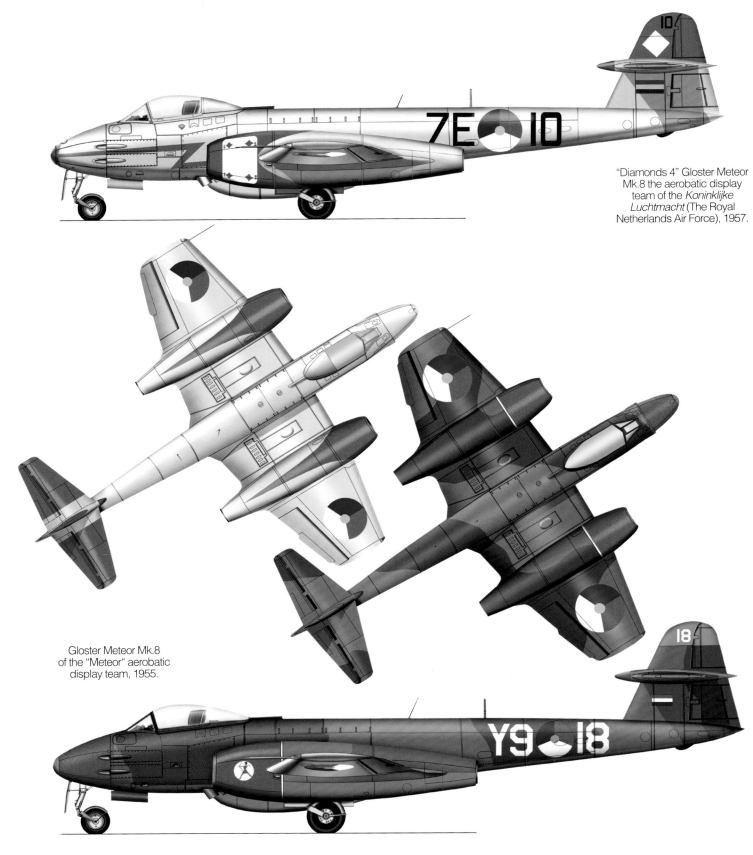

"Diamonds 4" Gloster Meteor Mk.8 the aerobatic display team of the *Koninklijke Luchtmacht* (The Royal Netherlands Air Force), 1957.

Gloster Meteor Mk.8 of the "Meteor" aerobatic display team, 1955.

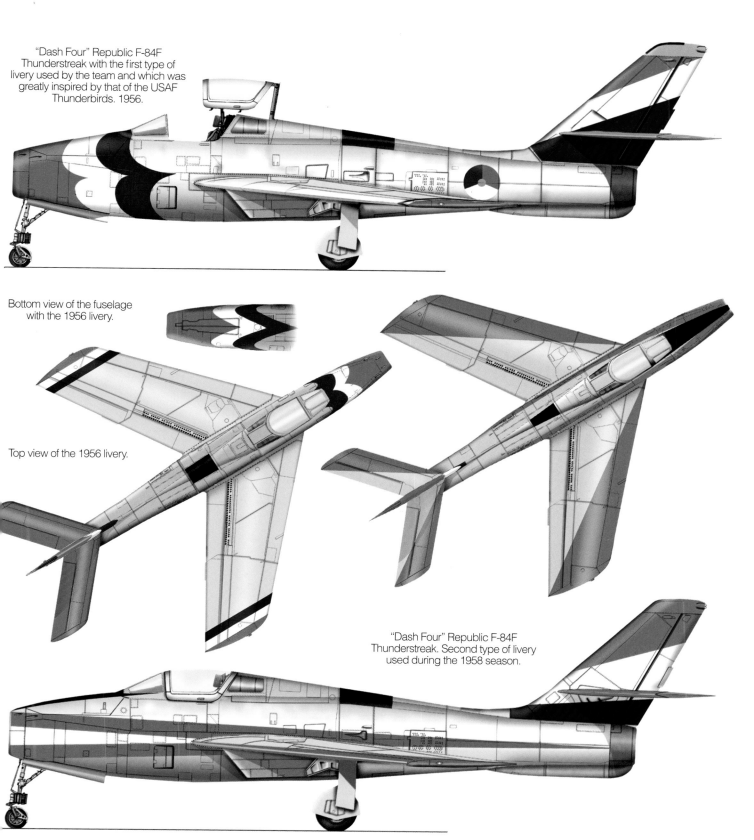

"Dash Four" Republic F-84F Thunderstreak with the first type of livery used by the team and which was greatly inspired by that of the USAF Thunderbirds. 1956.

Bottom view of the fuselage with the 1956 livery.

Top view of the 1956 livery.

"Dash Four" Republic F-84F Thunderstreak. Second type of livery used during the 1958 season.

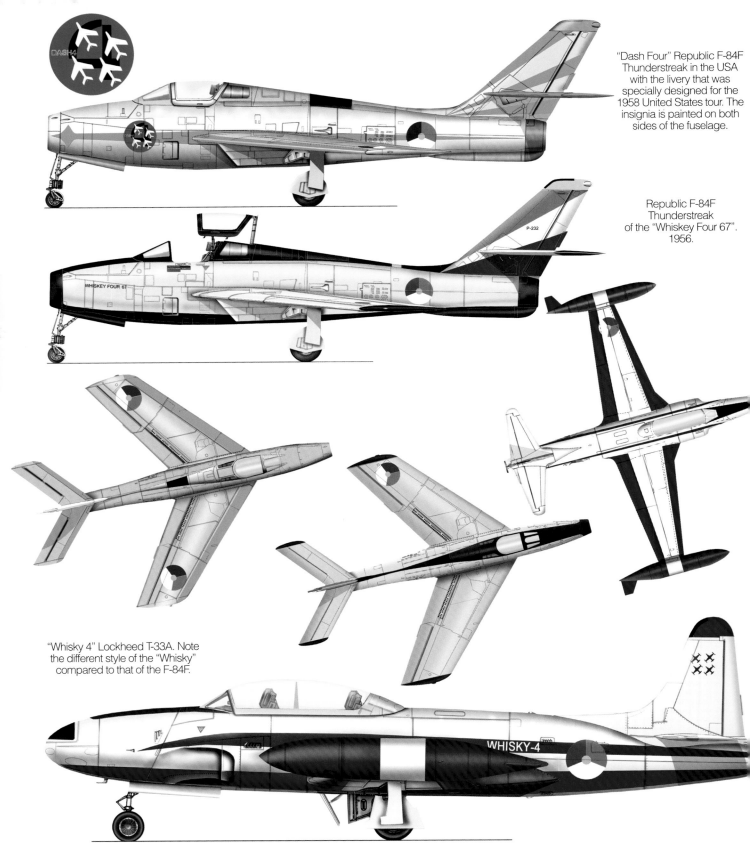

"Dash Four" Republic F-84F Thunderstreak in the USA with the livery that was specially designed for the 1958 United States tour. The insignia is painted on both sides of the fuselage.

Republic F-84F Thunderstreak of the "Whiskey Four 67". 1956.

"Whisky 4" Lockheed T-33A. Note the different style of the "Whisky" compared to that of the F-84F.

NORWAY

"Flying Jokers"

The "Flying Jokers" aerobatic display team was created in 1957 within 332 Skvadron of the *Norske Luftforsvaret* (Royal Norwegian Air Force) based at Rygge. The aircraft had no specific livery until the summer of 1959, when its six F-86F Sabre were painted in team colours, a livery which was used until the autumn of 1960, the year in which the F-86F was retired from service.

In June 1977, the "Flying Jokers" were part of 336 Skvadron, also based at Rygge and flew with four F-5A at the International Air Tattoo at Greenham Common, Great Britain. These aircraft bore the "Flying Jokers" insignia on the tail fin, but had no particular livery. This was the team's only display.

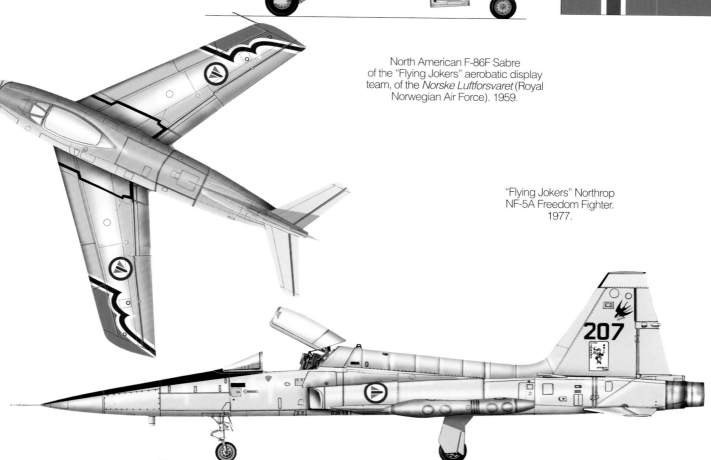

North American F-86F Sabre of the "Flying Jokers" aerobatic display team, of the *Norske Luftforsvaret* (Royal Norwegian Air Force). 1959.

"Flying Jokers" Northrop NF-5A Freedom Fighter. 1977.

PAKISTAN

"The Tigers"

"The Tigers" display team of the Combat Command School (CCS), *Pakistan Fiza'ya* (Pakistan Air Force), was created at the Sargodha air base in 1980. It was equipped with the F-6 (the Chinese version of the MiG-19), but only existed for a few months.

"The Sherdils"

The "Sherdils" were created on 17 August 1972 at the Risalpur air base. Equipped with four Cessna T-37 "Tweety

Bird", its pilots were instructors at the Basic Flying Training Wing. It was only when they began giving their first displays on 19 September 1974, that the team adopted the official name of "The Sherdils"; its four T-37 were entirely painted in red.

On 8 October 1978, during a training flight, Flight Lieutenant Alamdar Hussain collided in mid air with the pilot of n° 4 plane; the two aircraft crashed, killing both pilots. In 1980, two more planes were added to the team and the aircraft were given a livery consisting of white, red and blue, which is still in use today. In 2009, the T-37 were replaced with the K-8P Karakorum, the export version of the Chinese Hongdu JL-8.

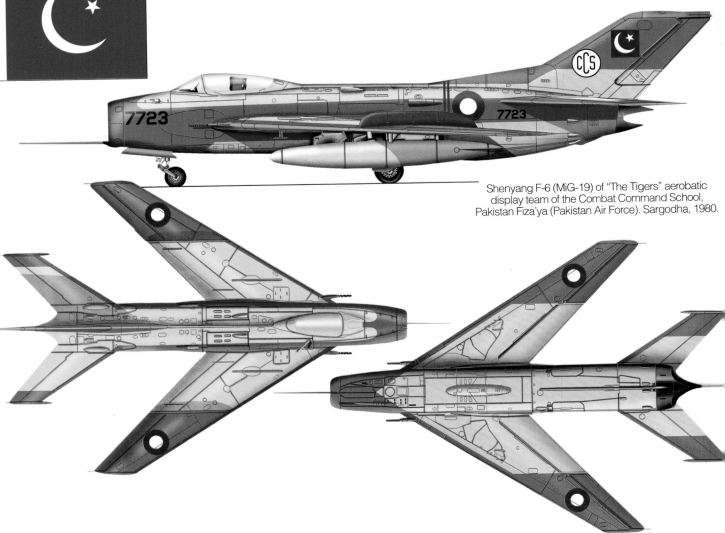

Shenyang F-6 (MiG-19) of "The Tigers" aerobatic display team of the Combat Command School, Pakistan Fiza'ya (Pakistan Air Force). Sargodha, 1980.

"The Sherdils" display team Cessna T-37C with the first type of livery. The lower surfaces are painted in the same way as the upper surfaces.

"The Sherdils" Cessna T-37C, 1975. Second type of livery.

PHILIPPINES

"The Blue Diamonds"

In 1958, the aerobatic team "The Blue Diamonds", formed within the 7th Tactical Fighter Squadron of the Philippine Air Force, changed its F-51D Mustangs for the F-86F Sabre. The team initially had eight aircraft, a number that increased to sixteen in 1960, the year in which pilots from other squadrons could apply to join the team. The following year, the number decreased to twelve aircraft, then nine in 1962.

The "Blue Diamonds" were disbanded in 1963 when the Philippine Air Force was sent to Africa as part of the United Nations intervention in Congo. At the end of these operations, the team was reformed with nine aircraft. The Sabres were replaced in 1965 by the Northrop F-5A Freedom Fighter. In 1971, the team only had five aircraft, a number later increased to six, then four F-5A in 1977, following the oil crisis.

Disbanded in 1978, the "Blue Diamonds" were reformed once more in 1986 until the Philippine Air Force decommissioned its F-5A aircraft in 2006.

North American F-86F Sabre of the "Blue Diamonds" aerobatic display team, Philippine Air Force. 1957.

"Blue Diamonds" Northrop F-5A, 1976.

POLAND

"Iskry"

The first aerobatic team of the *Ludowe Lotnictwo Polskie* (Polish Air Force, name changed to *Polska Wojska Lotnicze Obrony Powietrznej* after the collapse of the Eastern Bloc) was created at Radom air base on 16 February 1969. It was named "Rombik" (diamond) and equipped with four PZL TS-11 Iskra (Spark) training jets. The team carried out few displays with two solo planes, which did not have any special livery. The "Rombik" carried out their first public display on 17 August 1971, during the Polish Air Force Day at Deblin. The team was disbanded in 1981 and finally reformed in the spring of 1984, with its first display taking place the following 5 July at Poznan.

Renamed "Iskry" (sparks) in 1989, the team began flying in a six aircraft formation with one solo plane. In 1991, it was given the livery it uses to this day, with the white and red of the Polish flag. It first flew in public with this livery at the Poznan air show, then in Hungary the following 8 August and Belgium on 7 September.

In 1995, at the (Royal International Air Tattoo) at Fairford, Great Britain, the display team had a nine-plane formation and one solo. In 1998, the formation was eight planes with two solo. On 11 November of the same year, there was an accident involving plane n°5 which was carrying out a weather re-

connaissance ahead of the team's display over Warsaw. After flying for a few minutes in very bad weather, the plane crashed, killing the two pilots who were on board. Displays were stopped for two years following this accident.

Integrated into 1. *Osrodek Szkolenia Lotniczego* (Flight Training Centre n° 1) at the Deblin air base on 17 June 2000, the team changed its name to "Bialo-Czerwone Iskry" (white and red sparks) and was equipped with seven Iskra one of which was a solo plane.

On 1 September 2007, two of the team's planes collided during a display at Radom, killing the two pilots. In 2009, the "Iskry" carried out a display with four TS-11 Iskra at the Koksijde air show in Belgium.

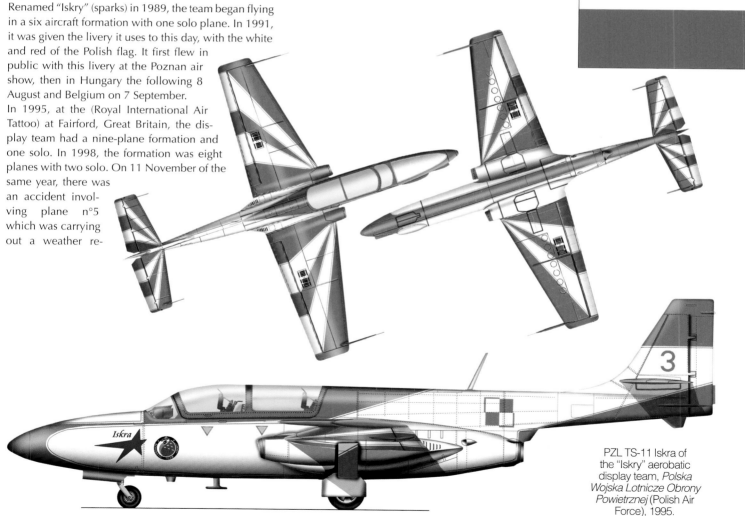

PZL TS-11 Iskra of the "Iskry" aerobatic display team, *Polska Wojska Lotnicze Obrony Powietrznej* (Polish Air Force), 1995.

PORTUGAL

"Asas de Portugal"

In order to show the Portuguese Air Force at the Royal International Air Tattoo in Great Britain, the commander-in-chief of the *Força Aerea Portuguesa* gave the order, in 1977, to form an aerobatic team within the 102a Esquadra "Panchos". Named "Asas de Portugal" (the wings of Portugal) and equipped with six Cessna T-37C, the team was disbanded in 1992 when the plane was retired from service. It had flown at 146 air shows and had carried out forty displays over Europe.

On 27 June 1997, a display team of 103a Esquadra "Caracois", equipped with Alpha Jets bought from Germany, took part in the show celebrating the 45th anniversary of the Portuguese Air Force at Sintra, west of Lisbon. The aircraft did not have a special livery at this time. This team was disbanded in 1998, with the Portuguese aviation fans calling for the return of the "Asas de Portugal". It was finally in 2005 that the "Asas de Portugal" were reformed as the official aerobatic team of the Força Aerea Portuguesa, depending on the 103a Esquadra, based at Beja, in the region of Alentejo and equipped with four Alpha Jet with a special livery. As a general rule, during air shows, the team, which is still flying, only uses two of its aircraft. Displays with all of its aircraft are uncommon.

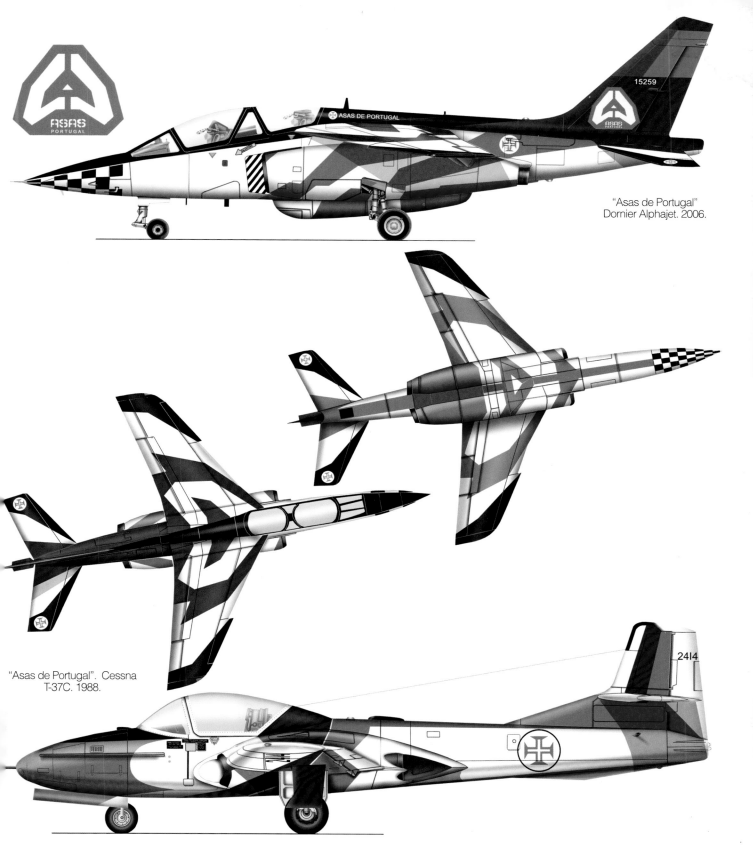

"Asas de Portugal"
Dornier Alphajet. 2006.

"Asas de Portugal". Cessna
T-37C. 1988.

1. PZL TS-II Iskra
of the «Iskry». *(THK)*
2 to 4. Dornier Alpha Jet
of the «Asas do Portugal».
(FAP)
5, 6, 8. Sukhoï Su-27S
and UB of the «Russkiye
Vityazi». *(DR)*
7. MIG. 29 «Fulcrums»
of the «Strizhi». *(DR)*

5

6

7

8

RUSSIAN FEDERATION

"Strizhi" (Swallows)

In 1986, the Soviet Union sent six of its new MiG-29 to take part in a display at an air show in Finland. After the success of this display, six pilots began close formation flying training, in 1990, with the Fulcrums which were given a special livery a short while after.

On 6 May 1991, the display team was named "Strizhi" (swallows) and in the days that followed, took part in an air show at Uppsala, in Sweden. A year later, the display team went to Reims, in France, for the 50th anniversary celebrations of the "Normandie-Niémen" squadron.

In 1993, the "Strizhi" were at LIMA 93, in Malaysia, as well as air shows in Thailand and Belgium. They also returned to Sweden in, and flew in Finland in 1997.

The team was disbanded in 1999, then reformed in 2000. On 23 November of the same year, based at Andreapol, it began flying with its new pilots with four planes. In 2001, the "Strizhi" flew their first public display at the Pushkino air base, near Saint-Petersburg.

In 2002, the "Strizhi" and the "Russkiye Vityazi" (Russian Knights), flew over Red Square, Moscow, as part of the fly past celebrating Russian Independence.

At the beginning of the new year, all of the team's planes were given a new livery and on 12 June 2003, Russian Independence day, four "Strizhi" Fulcrums, this time accompanied by four Su-27 of the "Russkiye Vityazi", flew once more over Red Square. On 27 July 2006, one of the team's two-seater MiG-29UB crashed shortly after take off at the Bolshoye Savino airport in the Ural, where the "Strizhi" had made a technical stopover, but the pilots were able to eject. Displays are usually carried out with formations of six MiG-29, a number that can sometimes be reduced for some shows. The "Strizhi" are still flying and are part of 237.

Mikoyan-Gourevitch MiG-29 "Fulcrum" of the "Strizhi" aerobatic display team, Russian Air Force, 1991.

Tsentr Pokaza Aviatsionnoy Tekhniki (TsPAT/Center for Display of Aviation Equipment) at the Kubinka air base.

44

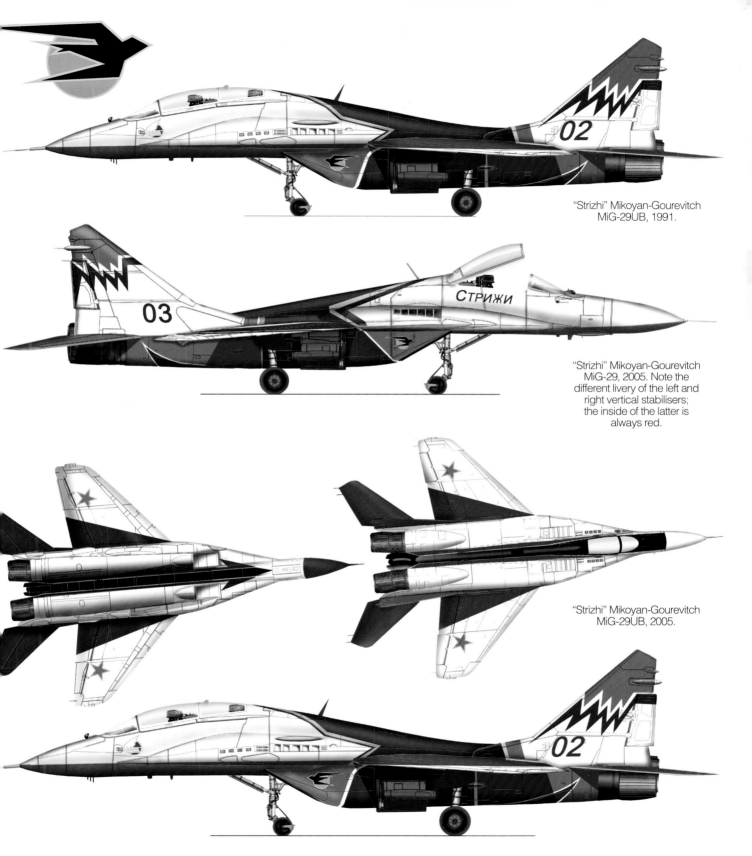

"Strizhi" Mikoyan-Gourevitch
MiG-29UB, 1991.

"Strizhi" Mikoyan-Gourevitch
MiG-29, 2005. Note the
different livery of the left and
right vertical stabilisers;
the inside of the latter is
always red.

"Strizhi" Mikoyan-Gourevitch
MiG-29UB, 2005.

Sukhoï Su-27S
of the "Russkiye Vityazi"
aerobatic display team, 2004.

"Russkiye Vityazi"
(Russian Knights)

The "Russkiye Vityazi" (Russian Knights) aerobatic
display team was formed within the *237. Tsentr Pokaza
Aviatsionnoy Tekhniki* (TsPAT/Center for Display of Aviation Equipment) at the Kubinka air base on 5 April 1991.
At the outset, it was equipped with three Sukhoï Su-27S
and three two-seater Su-27UB. It carried out its first overseas display in September 1991 during a visit to the "Red
Arrows" at Scampton (Great Britain). In

June
the fol-
lowing year, the
team flew in the USA
and Canada.

A terrible accident happened on 12 December 1995 when the formation, returning
from an air show in Malaysia, was preparing to land
for a stopover at the Kam-Ran air base in Vietnam.
The aircraft were guided by an Ilyouchine Il-76, but
following a navigational error, plus the very bad weather
conditions, the transport aircraft pilot led the formation
into a mountain. Three aircraft, two twin-seaters and a

single-seater, hit the mountain, killing the four pilots. The
rest of the formation and the transport aircraft managed to
avoid the mountain and landed at Kam-Ran.

Despite this loss, the "Russkiye Vityazi" flew once again
in 1996, but this time with a formation comprising of only
four aircraft.

On 21 June 1997, the team was arriving for an air show
at Bratislava, in Slovakia, when one of the planes made a
belly landing, its pilot having forgotten to lower his undercarriage…. The plane was quickly repaired and the
following day, the team carried out its displays with three
planes.

In 2002, the "Strizhi" and the "Russkiye Vityazi" began
training together in formations of four aircraft, each with
their own livery, for a flypast during the Red Square parade.

For the 65th anniversary of the Centre for Display of Aviation Equipment in March 2003, the two teams flew together once again, this time with ten aircraft, four Su-27
and six MiG-29. They did the same the following year
this time with a nine aircraft formation of five Su-27 and
four MiG-29.

On 16 August 2009, two "Russkiye Vityazi" aircraft, a Su-
27 and a Su-30, collided in mid air during a training flight
for the Moscow air show. Three of the pilots were able
to eject at low altitude, the crew of the two-seater Su-30
survived, but not the team leader whose parachute caught
fire when he ejected. The "Russkiye Vityazi" are still flying
and are attached to the 237. TsPAT at Kubinka.

"Russkiye Vityazi"
Sukhoï Su-27UB,
1994.

Mikoyan-Gourevitch
MiG-29S of the "Sokoly
Rossii" aerobatic display
team, 2006.

"Sokoly Rossii" (Russian Falcons)

The "Sokoly Rossii" (Russian Falcons) were formed at the Lipetsk air base in 2006 and equipped with specially painted MiG-29 and Su-27. It participated in the Zhukovsky international air show near Moscow on 20 August 2009.

"Nebesnyye Gusary" (Celestial Hussars)

Sukhoï Su-25 of the
"Nebesnyye Gusary"
aerobatic display team, 1996.

Also attached to the 237. TsPAT at Kubinka, the "Nebesnyye Gusary" (Celestial Hussars) display team was formed in 1994. It was supposed to have three types of plane at the beginning (Su-24M, Su-22 and Su-25), but the maintenance of these planes turned out to be complicated and the general staff finally decided to equip the team with four Su-25 "Frogfoot". The "Nebesnyye Gusary" were disbanded in 1997, after having only flown a few displays in Russia.

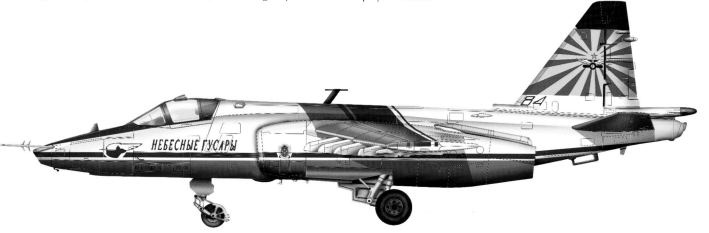

USSR

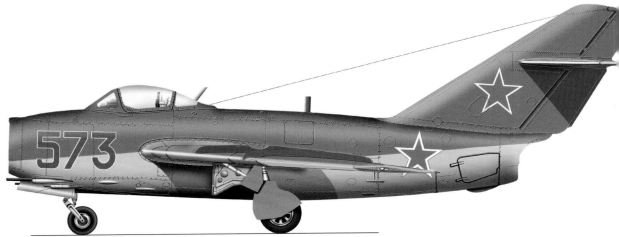

The creation of the Soviet Air Force in 1930, saw the formation of a display team whose aircraft, of various types, flew every time a parade was held in Red Square, or undertook displays over air bases.

The first aerobatic display team worthy of the name, was created at the beginning of the 1930s. Named the "Krasnaya Pyaterka" ("The Red Five"), it comprised of five red painted Polikarpov I-16, hence its name. Only the leader's plane retained its original green camouflage.

The Soviet display teams reappeared after the end of the Second World War, but only flew simple formation aerobatics during important events. The Yak-15, MiG-15 and MiG-21 were used in succession, with the upper surfaces painted red, the lower surfaces generally remaining in bare metal. However, some MiG-17 and MiG-19 had grey-blue lower surfaces. In general, the displays carried out by these teams lasted for 15 minutes. Apart from the "The Red Five", no other Soviet team had a name. Most of the aircraft were supplied by the176. IAP (Istrebitelniy Aviatsionniy Polk/fighter regi-

ment) based at Toplii Stan, near Moscow. In 1950, this unit was renamed 234. IAP and in 1952, the team was based at Kubinka. In 1989, the Regiment became the le 237. IAP and in 1992, it was named *237. Tsentr Pokaza Aviatsionnoy Tekhniki*. The last air display by a Soviet display team in the USSR took place at the Domodedovoen air base in 1967.

"The Red Five" aerobatic display team Mikoyan Gourevitch MiG-15 of the Soviet Air Force, Kubinka, 1950.

Mikoyan Gourevitch
MiG-17 of the Soviet Air Force
aerobatic display team, seen
here at Koubinka prior to
1955.

Mikoyan Gourevitch MiG-17
of the Soviet Air Force seen at
Koubinka prior to 1955.

Mikoyan Gourevitch
MiG-19S of the Soviet Air
Force aerobatic display team,
end of the 1950s.

Mikoyan Gourevitch MiG-21
PFM of the Soviet Air Force
aerobatic display team, 1967.

SAUDI ARABIA

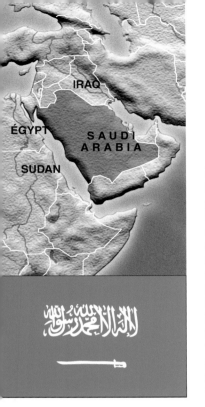

"The Saudi Hawks"

In 1988-1989, six Hawk Mk.65 ordered by Saudi Arabia, were modified by British Aerospace at Warton and given smoke generators. A little while after, the last six Hawks of the second delivery batch bought by the Saudis (second generation), were also given smoke generators. However, all of these aircraft retained their standard camouflage scheme used by the Al Quwwat al Jawwiya as Sa'udiya (Royal saudi Air Force or RSAF).

It was at the King Abdul Aziz air base, on June 1998, that No 88 Squadron was officially created and named "RSAF Display Team". Its main role consisted of representing the RSAF during national and international events.

Three first generation Hawk Mk.65 and all of the second generation Mk.65A were transferred to the new squadron in February-March 1999, giving the team a total of nine aircraft.

During a formation training flight on 27 September 1998, n° 7915, still bearing its original camouflage, overran the runway and its pilot was forced to eject.

The team received its new green and white livery, the colours of the national roundel, in October 1998 and left the King Abdul Aziz air base for that of King Faisal at Tabuk in February 1999, alongside the other Hawk equipped squadrons of the RSAF.

The team carried out its first display in the same year at Riyad, the Kingdom's capital, during the 100th anniversary celebrations of the creation of Saudi Arabia.

In February 2000, the "Saudi Hawks" flew at Bahrain and, on 5 February 2002, two planes collided whilst the formation was landing and the two pilots were able to eject.

On 24 July 2005, another plane was lost during a display and once gain the pilots were able to eject. The Saudi Hawks are still flying and took part in the Ain Airport air show in the United Arab Emirates, in 2009.

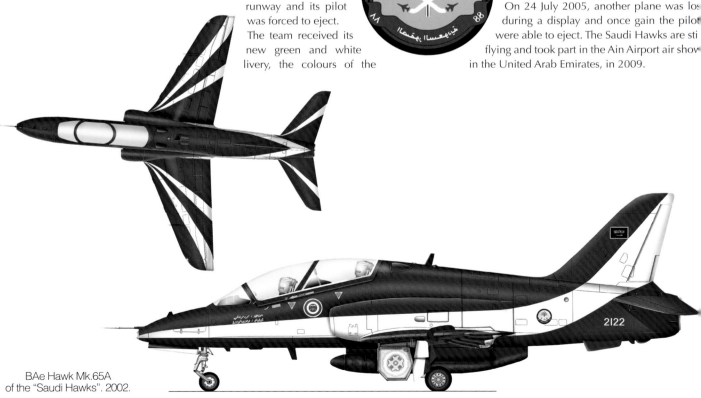

BAe Hawk Mk.65A
of the "Saudi Hawks". 2002.

SINGAPORE

"The Black Knights"

The "Black Knights", the aerobatic display team of the Republic of Singapore Air Force (RSAF) was created in 1973 and carried out its first display on the RSAF Day at Changi air base on 7 June 1976. At this time, they were equipped with four Hawker Hunters, a plane that was used until 1983.

Another display team, the "Flying Tigers", equipped with five F-5E Tiger II, was created in 1981. After the last display given by the "Black Knights" with their Hunters, the "Flying Tigers" were renamed the "Black Knights" and thus became the RSAF's sole display team.

At this time, neither the Hunters, nor the Tiger II were specifically attached to the team and did not, therefore, have the white and red livery that was later officially adopted by the "Black Knights".

In 1990, the team, now dedicated solely to flying displays, comprised of six Douglas A-4SU Super Skyhawks, an improved version of the famous Skyhawk, notably equipped with a better jet engine.

Two F-16 were attached to the team in 1999 and the "Black Knights" thus became the only display team to use two types of plane, these being four A-4SU and two F-16A. Their first air show in this configuration took place at the Asian Aerospace Exhibition held at the Changi airbase, Singapore, in February 2000.

In the autumn of 2007, the "Black Knights" only had F-16, with which they flew at the Singapore Aerospace Exhibitionon 19 February 2008, before taking part, the following 24 April, in an air show at Bangkok in Thailand, but with only five aircraft, as number 4 had been damaged in between the two shows.

This display team does not carry out many displays, but was still flying in 2009.

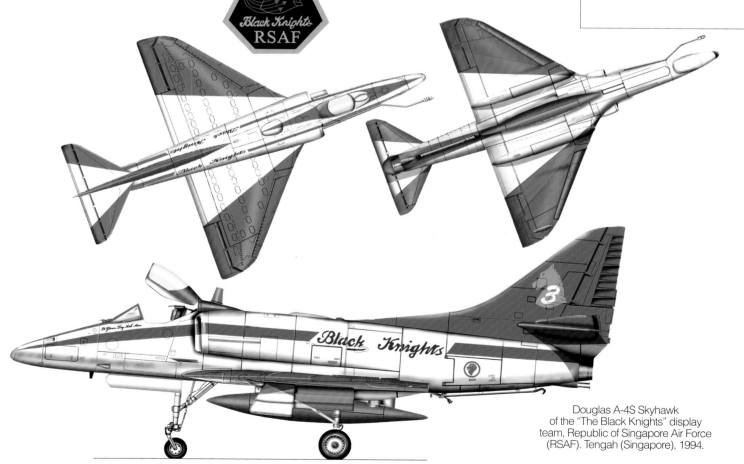

Douglas A-4S Skyhawk
of the "The Black Knights" display team, Republic of Singapore Air Force (RSAF). Tengah (Singapore), 1994.

"Black Knights" LMTAS F-16C
Fighting Falcon, Tengah,
2008.

SLOVAKIA

"Biele Albatrosy" (White Albatrosses)

The "Biele Albatrosy" (White Albatrosses) display team of the *Velitelstvo Vzdusnych Sil* (Slovakian Air Force), was created at the beginning of 1991, when three L-39 Albatross (Czech made training aircraft) made a fly past at the opening ceremony of the 9th World Parachuting Championship at the Lucenec-Bolkovce airfield, on 3 August 1991. When this base was modernised, the unit temporarily set up home at Prerov in 1992 where it flew its first display with six L-39, at the Moravian-Silesian Region air show.

The "Biele Albatrosy" display team was attached to the Slovakian Air Force in 1993 following the "Velvet Revolution", where Czechoslovakia split into the two sovereign countries of the Czech Republic and Slovakia.

In 1994, the "Biele Albatrosy" flew in Denmark, Great Britain and Hungary, and in the following year, a seventh plane was added to the team.

A serious accident happened on 17 July 1996, when planes n° 2 and n° 6 collided in mid air during a training flight. N° 2 crashed, although the two

pilots managed to eject, whilst n° 6 was able to make an emergency landing.

The team returned to its original base at Kocice in 1997.

There was another accident on 3 June 2000 at the Sliac air show, this time involving

Albatros n° 3 which hit the ground, killing its pilot.

In 2001, the "Biele Albatrosy" only had five aircraft and the team was disbanded at the end of the year.

Throughout their career, the "Biele Albatrosy" were accompanied by an Antonov An-26 transport plane with the same livery as those of the team's jets.

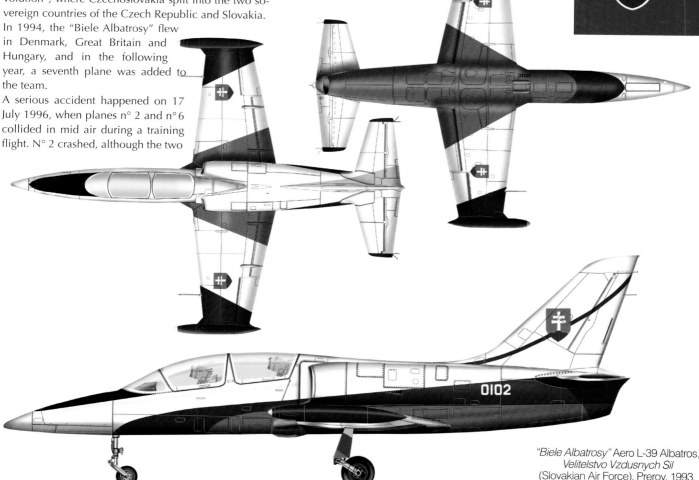

"Biele Albatrosy" Aero L-39 Albatros, *Velitelstvo Vzdusnych Sil* (Slovakian Air Force). Prerov, 1993.

SOUTH AFRICA

"The Silver Falcons"

In 1966, the South African Atlas Aircraft Corporation delivered to the Central Flying School of the South African Air Force (SAAF) Impala Mk.1 training jets, the built under licence version of the Aermacchi MB 326. A short while later, the school's staff officers decided to form a display team equipped with these new planes.

The team made its first public display on 24 November 1967, during the opening ceremony of the Atlas Aircraft Corporation, and was named a short while later the "Silver Falcons" ("Silwer Valke" in Afrikaans). In 1985, the planes were given a new livery of silver, white, orange and blue; based on the colours of the national flag at the time, as well as yellow numbers 1 to 4. In 1988, a fifth plane was added to the team.

During an air show at Lanseria airport on le 2 October 1993, plane n°5 crashed due to a structural fault when its right wing came off. The pilot managed to eject seconds before the plane crashed, but was killed. In 1994, the "Silver Falcons" changed colours again, this time to silver, blue, white and light blue; the team also received at this time a sixth plane.

The SAAF celebrated its 75th anniversary in 1995 and the "Silver Falcons" were attached to the 85th Combat Flying School at the Hoedspruit air base, before finally being disbanded at the end of the same year.

The "Silver Falcons" were reformed in 1999, this time within the Central Flying School at Langebaanweg, but equipped with four turbine powered Pilatus PC-7 Mk. 2 Astras.

Aermacchi MB-326H Impala of the "Silver Falcons" display team, South African Air Force, 1982.

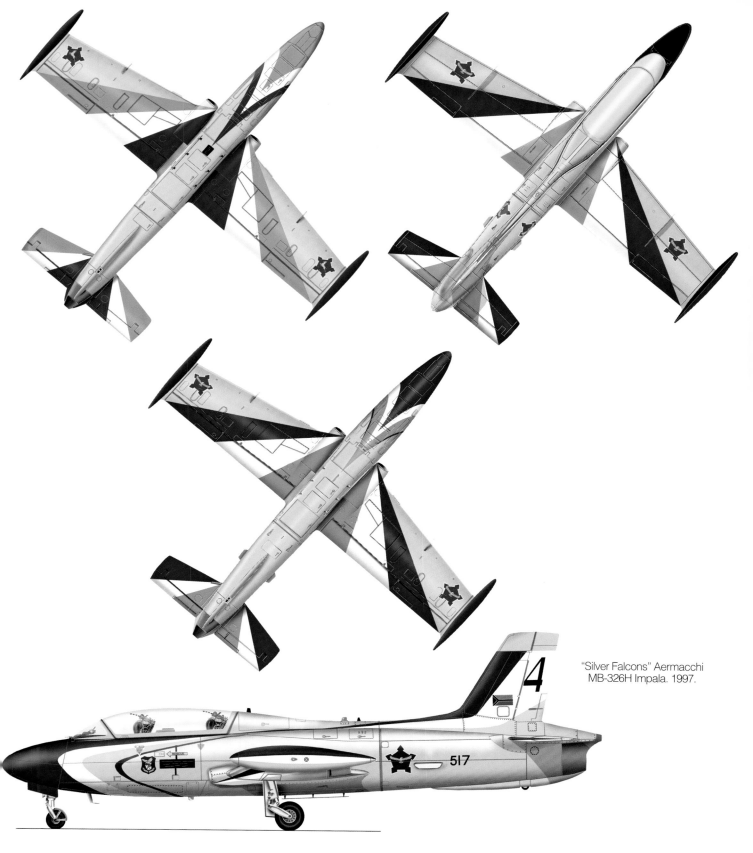

"Silver Falcons" Aermacchi MB-326H Impala. 1997.

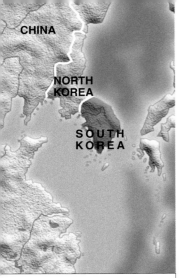

SOUTH KOREA

"The Black Eagles"

The "Black Eagles" began flying as the display team of the *Han Guk Gong Gun* (Republic of Korea Air Force or Ro-KAF) on 12 December 1994. At this time, it was equipped with six Cessna A-37B Dragonfly and attached to the 239th Special Flying Squadron of the 8th Fighter Wing based at Wonju. The "Black Eagles" carried out their first display on 25 September 1995.

On 8 May 1998, two of the team's planes collided during a training flight, with the lea-der's plane crashing and killing its pilot, whereas the other plane, having only suffered superficial damage, managed to land. Another fatal accident occurred on 5 May 2006 during the Seoul air show when one of the team's planes crashed, killing the pilot. At the end of the 2007 season, the "Black Eagles" were temporarily disbanded after the RoKAF's A-37 aircraft were retired from service.

The team was reformed in 2010, after having received the first Korean made trai-ning jet, the KAI (Korea Aerospace Indus-try) T-50B Golden Eagle.

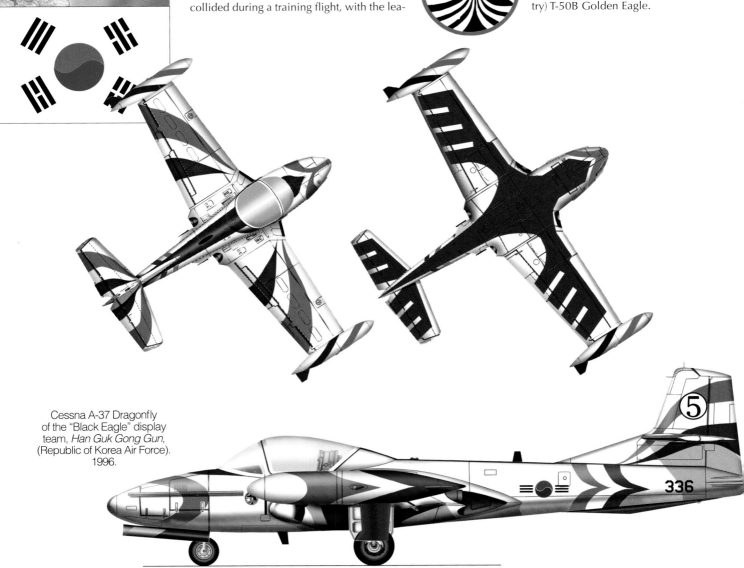

Cessna A-37 Dragonfly of the "Black Eagle" display team, *Han Guk Gong Gun*, (Republic of Korea Air Force). 1996.

SPAIN

"Patrulla Ascua"

During a training flight in 1956, the leader of a formation of four F-86 Sabres decided to carry out some aerobatics. This was the beginning of the display team that two years later would be known under the official name of "Patrulla Ascua "(lit. ember patrol)

A fifth Sabre was added to the team, at the time part of the *Ala de Caza n° 1* (1st fighter squadron) based at Manises. Their first display was on 23 February 1956 at Manises and on the following 22 June, they flew at Rome to celebrate the opening of a new airport. The aircraft were painted red and yellow for the latter display, the colours of the Spanish flag.

During a training flight on 28 September 1958, n°4 crashed and this accident led to the team stopping its displays until 2 May 1962, the date upon which it left for Seville; it then took part in several air shows. On 12 January 1965, the "Patrulla Ascua" carried out its last display.

"Patrulla Aguila"

The *Ejército Del Aire* (Spanish Air Force) deemed its CASA C-101 Aviojets capable of flying in close formation in order to create a national display team named the "Patrulla Aguila" (Eagle Patrol) whose pilots came from the Academia General del Aire (Air Academy) of San Javier.

On 14 June 1985, the team flew its first public display with four C-101 at the Jerez de la Frontera air base. At this time, the planes were painted silver and bore their formation insignia. For their second display, the "Eagles" had five aircraft, a number that was increased to six for the third display.

The first overseas displays took place in Belgium in 1886 and in Great Britain in 1987 at the Royal Air Tattoo.

On 11 April 1988, the Spanish king and queen watched a display at the Academia General del Aire of San Javier. In October 1991, the team received the livery it uses to this day, which is reminiscent of the livery previously used by the "Patrulla Ascua". A little later, during the summer of 1992, the team took part in the opening ceremony for the Barcelona Olympics. The "Patrulla Aguila" still flies today.

North American F-86F Sabre of the "Ascua" display team. Ala de Caza n° 1, Ejercito del Aire (Spanish Air Force). 1963-1964. First livery.

"Patrulla Ascua" North American F-86F Sabre. Second livery.

C5-199

1-199

CASA C-101 Aviojet of the «Patrulla Aguila». 2001.

79-11

Above and opposite.
CASA C. 101 Aviojet of the «Patrulla Aguila». *(G. Paloque Coll.)*

ottom.
ew type of livery worn with reduced
odes and rudder flag. *(EdA)*

SWEDEN

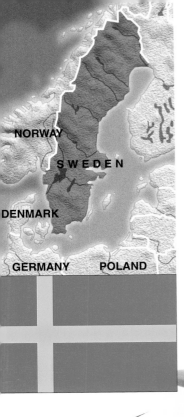

Acro Hunters, Acro Deltas, Vikings, Team 60

The Swedish aerobatic display teams started flying again with jets with the "Flying Barrels", a team equipped with four SAAB J29 Tunnan that had no special livery, then with the "Acro Hunters" with the Hawker Hunter, a team that flew in 1960- 1961 and finally with the "Acro Deltas" with the SAAB 35 Draken, a team that flew in 1964 and 1965.

In 1967, the *Svenska Flygvapnet* (Swedish Air Force) created an unofficial display team in order to promote the new Swedish built SAAB 105 training jet at the Le Bourget air show in France.

Another team, the "Team 60" (its name came from the Swedish SK 60 designation of the SAAB 105) was created in 1973, taking over from the "Vikings" that existed until 1968. In 1974, the team became official, was equipped with four jets and attached to the Ljungbyhed flying school in southern Sweden.

In 1975, two more planes were attached to "Team 60", which carried out its first public display with this formation in May 1976 at Göteborg. Since this date, the team has carried out displays in Sweden and a few in other countries.

Hawker Hunter Mk.6 of the "Acro Hunters" display team, *Svenska Flygvapnet* (Swedish Air Force), 1956.

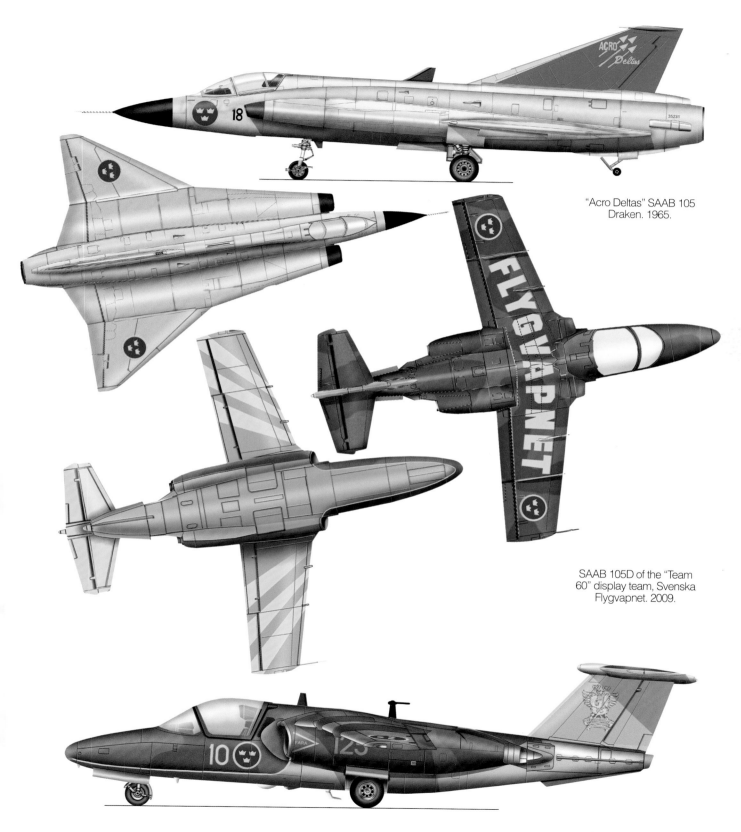

"Acro Deltas" SAAB 105
Draken. 1965.

SAAB 105D of the "Team
60" display team, Svenska
Flygvapnet. 2009.

SWITZERLAND

"Patrouille Suisse"

The "Patrouille Suisse", equipped with four Hawker Hunter Mk.58, made its first public appearance on 2 June 1959 at Biel, but its display was devoid of any aerobatics. Its first real display took place at Berne in 1963, during the "Oskar Bider" Day, celebrating one of the pioneers of Swiss aviation.
It was in 1964 that the team officially adopted its name of "Patrouille Suisse" during a display at Lausanne. It then flew at the 50th anniversary of the Swiss Air Forces (Schweizer Luftwaffe) at Dudendorf. The pilots came from the 1st and 11th squadrons of the Swiss Air Force and trained in their own free time.
In 1968, there was an attempt to form a team with the Mirage IIIS, but these aircraft proved difficult to fly in close formation.

A Hawker Hunter was added to the team in 1970. Th[e] "Patrouille Suisse" gave displays in Switzerland un[til] 1978, the year in which it received a sixth plane. [It] then took part in the 25th anniversary celebrations [of] the Patrouille de France which took place at Salon-de[-] Provence on 9 July 1978.

In 1991, the Swiss flag was painted unde[r] neath the fuselage, as up to that point, th[e] "Patrouille Suisse" had flown with a sta[n] dard camouflage scheme. The team's [fi] nal display with the Hawker Hunters too[k] place at Nancy in France on 25 Septemb[er] 1994. In June the following year, they fle[w] with the F-5E Tiger II, these planes having bee[n] given a special livery.

In 1996, the Swiss astronaut Claude Nico[l] lier, a former pilot with the team, was part [of] the crew of the Columbia space shuttle an[d] wore the team's insignia on his space suit. During the 1998 football world cup, t[he] team made a flypast over Paris. The same ye[ar] the pilot of n° 4 was killed whilst flying a F/A-[18] Hornet, which explains why this plane bor[e] grey livery until the end of the season.

In 1999, the "Patrouille Suisse" did not car[ry] out any displays due to the war in former Yug[o] lavia. In 2009, it celebrated its 45th anniversary a[nd] its tenth season flying the F-5E. The "Patrouille Suiss[e]" still flies today.

"Patrouille Suisse" Hawker Hunter F-58 with special livery celebrating the team's 30th anniversary. 1990.

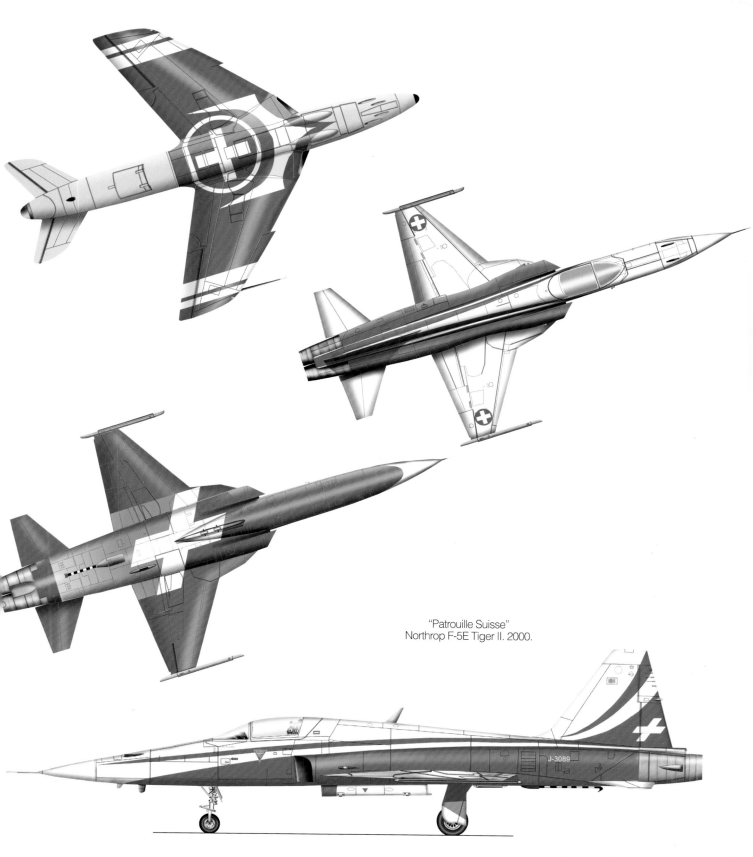

"Patrouille Suisse"
Northrop F-5E Tiger II. 2000.

J-3089

TURKEY

"Uçan Kugular "(Flying Swans)

The display team of the *Türk Hava Kuvvetleri* (Turkish Air Force) was formed at N° 4 air base at Eskisehir in 1955. Equipped with the F-86E Sabre, it was named the" Uçan Kugular "(Flying Swans) and existed until 1965. All of the planes had a special livery and flew in a nine, or twelve aircraft formation, but only carried out displays in Turkey.

"Türk Yildizlari "(Turkish Stars)

This display team was created at the end of 1992 and named "Türk Yildizlari "(Turkish Stars) on 11 January

the following year. It belonged to the 132 Filo (squadron) of the 3ncu AJÜ (Ana Jet Üs/3rd air squadron) based at Konya.

It carried out its first display in 1994 at Diyarbekir. At the beginning, the team comprised of seven F-5 and in 2001, it was one of the rare aerobatic teams made up of eight supersonic jets.

The "Türk Yildizlari "originally had a Lockheed C-130 Hercules support aircraft painted in the team's colours, a plane which was replaced in 2008 by a C.160 Transall.

Today, the team has seven single seat NF-5A and two twin-seater NF-5B.

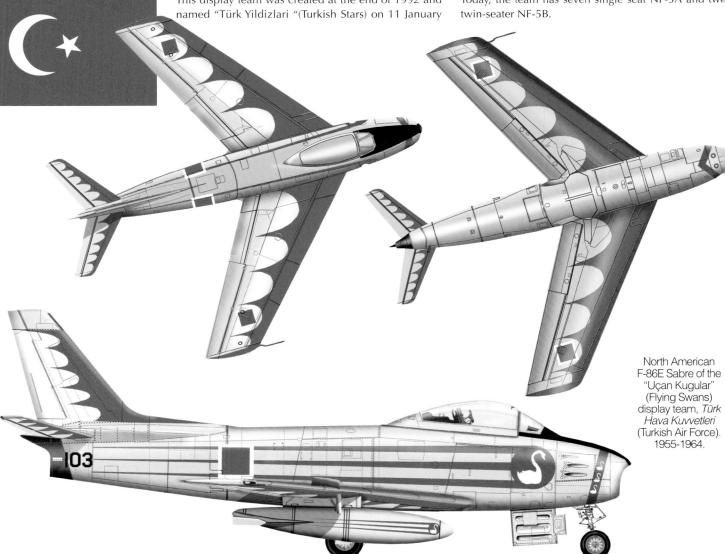

North American F-86E Sabre of the "Uçan Kugular" (Flying Swans) display team, *Türk Hava Kuvvetleri* (Turkish Air Force). 1955-1964.

Northrop F-5E Tiger II
of the "Türk Yildizlari"
(Turkish Stars), THK. 1998.

Northrop F-5B
of the "Türk Yildizlari"
(Turkish Stars), THK. 1998.

1. Northrop F-5E Tiger of the «Patrouille suisse». *(G. Paloque Coll.)*

2. Hawker Hunter F-Mark 58 of the «Patrouille suisse». *(G. Paloque Coll.)*

3. Northrop F-5E Tiger II of the «Türk Yildizlari» (Turkish Stars). *(THK)*

4

5

4. Northrop F-5B
of the « Türk Yildizlari ».
(THK)

5. MIG 29S of the
« Ukraizins'ki Sokoly »
(Ukrainians falcons).

6. SAAB 105D
(SK-60)
of the « Team 60 ».
(Svenska Flygvapnet)

6

UKRAINE

"Ukrayins'ki Sokoly" (Ukrainian Falcons)

When the *Povitryani Syly Ukrayiny* (Ukrainian Air Force) was created in 1992, it sent two MiG-29 (a single and twin-seater) to carry out displays at numerous European and North American bases. These MiG-29 bore the national colours of blue and yellow.

It was only in 1997 that the "Ukrayins'ki Sokoly" (Ukrainian Falcons) display team was created at the Kirov air base in East Crimea. The team, at this time, had six MiG-29. Its international debut was at the Royal International Tattoo at Fairford, in Great Britain in July 1997 with a formation of six single seat MiG-29B and twin-seater MiG-29UB.

On 26 March 1998, one of the team's MiG-29 crashed on landing at the Kirov air base during a training flight held in bad weather conditions, for a display that was to take place in France in May; the pilot was killed. Following this accident, the "Ukrayins'ki Sokoly" were disbanded for the remainder of the 1998 season and today, its status has not been decided.

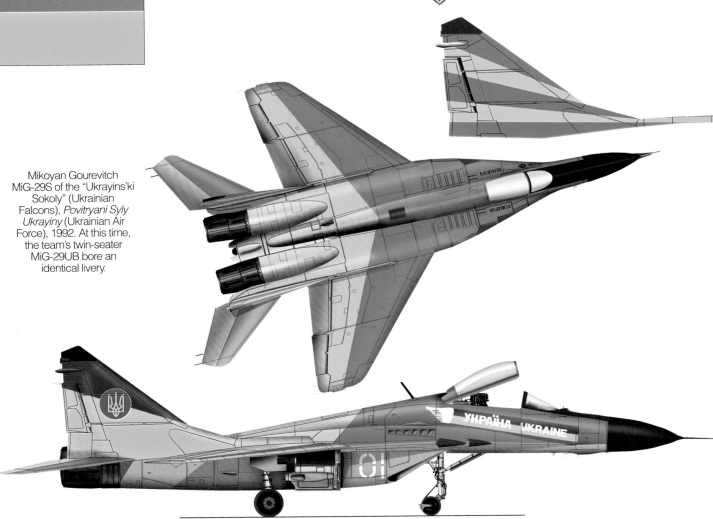

Mikoyan Gourevitch MiG-29S of the "Ukrayins'ki Sokoly" (Ukrainian Falcons), *Povitryani Syly Ukrayiny* (Ukrainian Air Force), 1992. At this time, the team's twin-seater MiG-29UB bore an identical livery.

Mikoyan Gourevitch MiG-29S
of the "Ukrayins'ki Sokoly"
(Ukrainian Falcons). 1997.

UKRANIAN FALCONS

102

UNITED KINGDOM

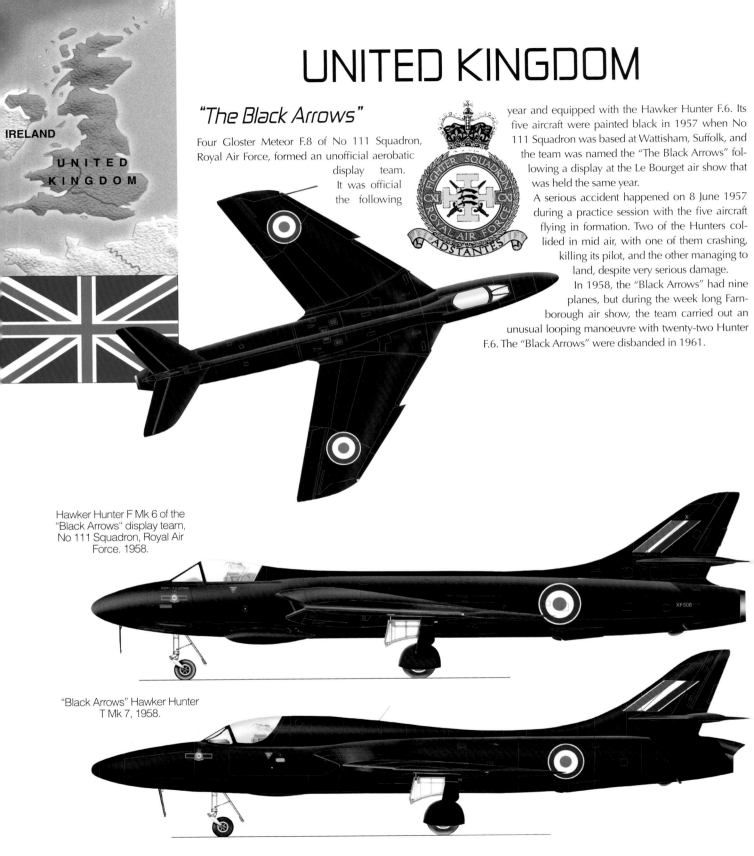

"The Black Arrows"

Four Gloster Meteor F.8 of No 111 Squadron, Royal Air Force, formed an unofficial aerobatic display team. It was official the following year and equipped with the Hawker Hunter F.6. Its five aircraft were painted black in 1957 when No 111 Squadron was based at Wattisham, Suffolk, and the team was named the "The Black Arrows" following a display at the Le Bourget air show that was held the same year.

A serious accident happened on 8 June 1957 during a practice session with the five aircraft flying in formation. Two of the Hunters collided in mid air, with one of them crashing, killing its pilot, and the other managing to land, despite very serious damage.

In 1958, the "Black Arrows" had nine planes, but during the week long Farnborough air show, the team carried out an unusual looping manoeuvre with twenty-two Hunter F.6. The "Black Arrows" were disbanded in 1961.

Hawker Hunter F Mk 6 of the "Black Arrows" display team, No 111 Squadron, Royal Air Force. 1958.

"Black Arrows" Hawker Hunter T Mk 7, 1958.

"The Blue Diamonds"

Following the disbanding of the "Black Arrows", a new display team, the "Blue Diamonds" was created within No 92 Squadron, RAF based at Middleton St. George and equipped with Hawker Hunters. The team carried on the traditions of the "Black Arrows", but in a diffe-

rent way, with its sixteen planes splitting into two groups during displays, one with nine planes, the other with seven. The Hawker Hunter F.6 and T-7 (two-seater) of No 92 Squadron were painted blue with a white lightning stripe running along the entire length of the fuselage. The "Blue Diamonds" took part in the 1961 and 1962 seasons.

Hawker Hunter F Mk.6 of the "The Blue Diamonds" aerobatic display team, No 92 Squadron, RAF. 1961-1962.

"Blue Diamonds" Hawker Hunter T Mk 7, 1962.

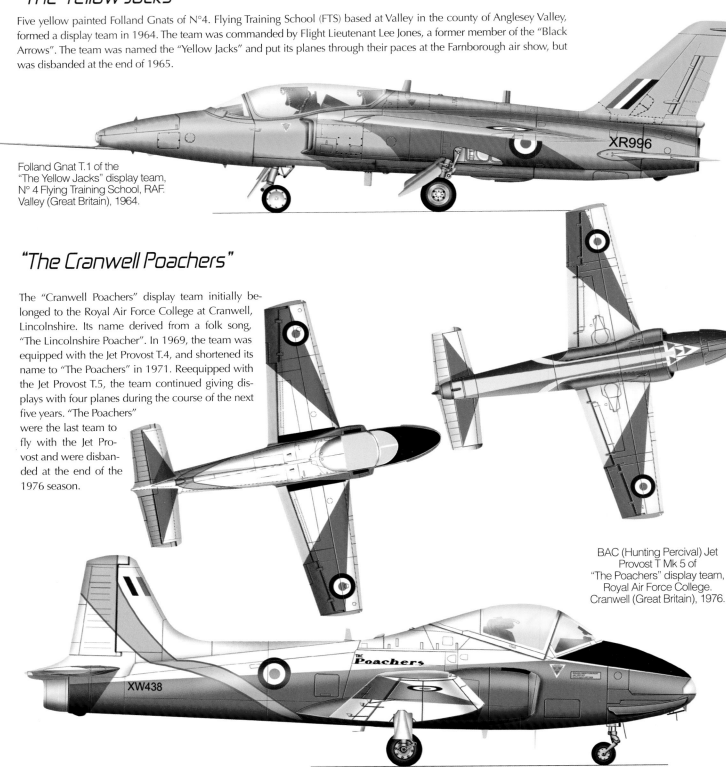

"The Yellow Jacks"

Five yellow painted Folland Gnats of N°4. Flying Training School (FTS) based at Valley in the county of Anglesey Valley, formed a display team in 1964. The team was commanded by Flight Lieutenant Lee Jones, a former member of the "Black Arrows". The team was named the "Yellow Jacks" and put its planes through their paces at the Farnborough air show, but was disbanded at the end of 1965.

Folland Gnat T.1 of the
"The Yellow Jacks" display team,
N° 4 Flying Training School, RAF.
Valley (Great Britain), 1964.

"The Cranwell Poachers"

The "Cranwell Poachers" display team initially belonged to the Royal Air Force College at Cranwell, Lincolnshire. Its name derived from a folk song, "The Lincolnshire Poacher". In 1969, the team was equipped with the Jet Provost T.4, and shortened its name to "The Poachers" in 1971. Reequipped with the Jet Provost T.5, the team continued giving displays with four planes during the course of the next five years. "The Poachers" were the last team to fly with the Jet Provost and were disbanded at the end of the 1976 season.

BAC (Hunting Percival) Jet
Provost T Mk 5 of
"The Poachers" display team,
Royal Air Force College.
Cranwell (Great Britain), 1976.

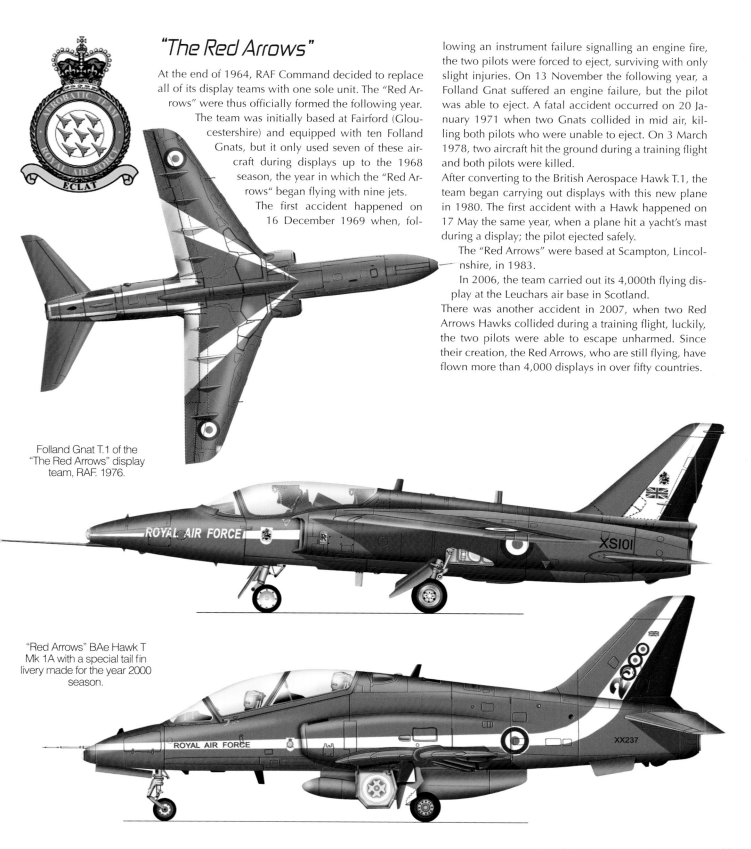

"The Red Arrows"

At the end of 1964, RAF Command decided to replace all of its display teams with one sole unit. The "Red Arrows" were thus officially formed the following year. The team was initially based at Fairford (Gloucestershire) and equipped with ten Folland Gnats, but it only used seven of these aircraft during displays up to the 1968 season, the year in which the "Red Arrows" began flying with nine jets.

The first accident happened on 16 December 1969 when, following an instrument failure signalling an engine fire, the two pilots were forced to eject, surviving with only slight injuries. On 13 November the following year, a Folland Gnat suffered an engine failure, but the pilot was able to eject. A fatal accident occurred on 20 January 1971 when two Gnats collided in mid air, killing both pilots who were unable to eject. On 3 March 1978, two aircraft hit the ground during a training flight and both pilots were killed.

After converting to the British Aerospace Hawk T.1, the team began carrying out displays with this new plane in 1980. The first accident with a Hawk happened on 17 May the same year, when a plane hit a yacht's mast during a display; the pilot ejected safely.

The "Red Arrows" were based at Scampton, Lincolnshire, in 1983.

In 2006, the team carried out its 4,000th flying display at the Leuchars air base in Scotland.

There was another accident in 2007, when two Red Arrows Hawks collided during a training flight, luckily, the two pilots were able to escape unharmed. Since their creation, the Red Arrows, who are still flying, have flown more than 4,000 displays in over fifty countries.

Folland Gnat T.1 of the "The Red Arrows" display team, RAF. 1976.

"Red Arrows" BAe Hawk T Mk 1A with a special tail fin livery made for the year 2000 season.

(RAF/Red Arrows)

(G. Paloque Coll.)

(G. Paloque Coll.)

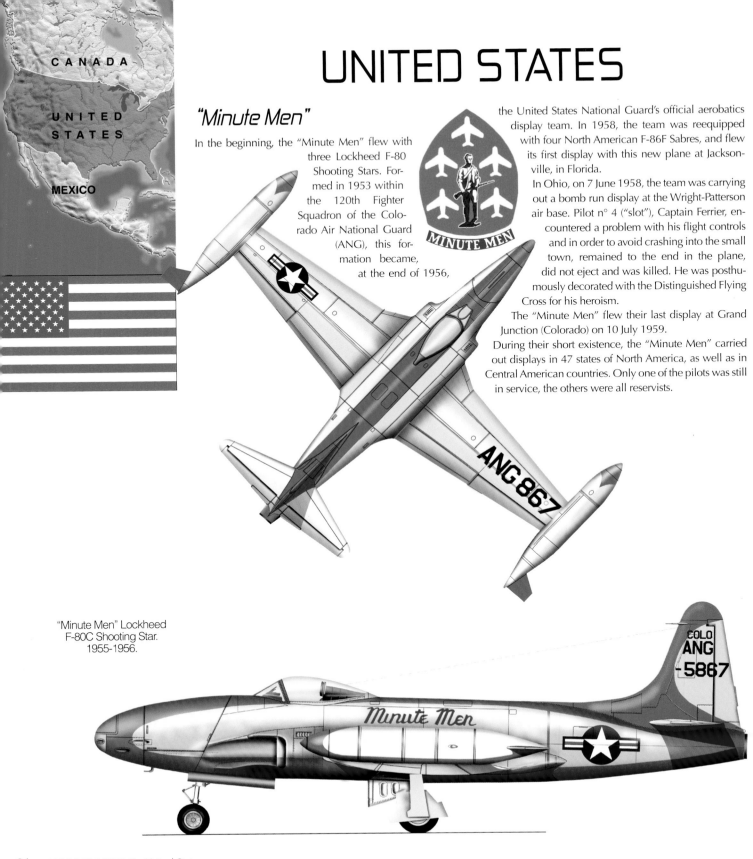

"Minute Men"

In the beginning, the "Minute Men" flew with three Lockheed F-80 Shooting Stars. Formed in 1953 within the 120th Fighter Squadron of the Colorado Air National Guard (ANG), this formation became, at the end of 1956, the United States National Guard's official aerobatics display team. In 1958, the team was reequipped with four North American F-86F Sabres, and flew its first display with this new plane at Jacksonville, in Florida.

In Ohio, on 7 June 1958, the team was carrying out a bomb run display at the Wright-Patterson air base. Pilot n° 4 ("slot"), Captain Ferrier, encountered a problem with his flight controls and in order to avoid crashing into the small town, remained to the end in the plane, did not eject and was killed. He was posthumously decorated with the Distinguished Flying Cross for his heroism.

The "Minute Men" flew their last display at Grand Junction (Colorado) on 10 July 1959.

During their short existence, the "Minute Men" carried out displays in 47 states of North America, as well as in Central American countries. Only one of the pilots was still in service, the others were all reservists.

"Minute Men" Lockheed
F-80C Shooting Star.
1955-1956.

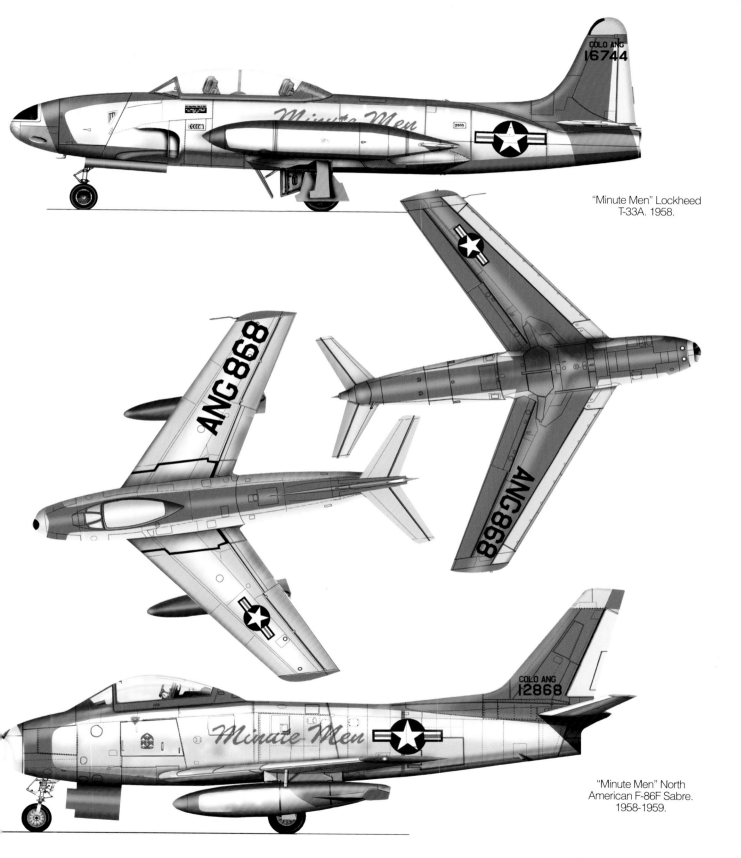

"Minute Men" Lockheed
T-33A. 1958.

"Minute Men" North
American F-86F Sabre.
1958-1959.

"Skyblazers"

Several flying instructors of the 22nd Fighter Squadron, 36th Fighter Wing based at Fürstenfeldbruck, Bavaria, were in the habit of flying formation aerobatics with their Lockheed F-80B "Shooting Stars" at the beginning of 1949 and were, therefore, at the origin of the US Air Force Europe (USAFE) aerobatics display team, the "Skyblazers".

In May 1949, the USAFE general staff officially asked the 36th Wing to form a display team equipped with the F-80B in order to fly at displays all over Europe and the North African continent. The "Skyblazers" flew their first display in October 1949 at RAF Gütersloh, in Germany, thus becoming the second USAF display team equipped with jets.

The 36th Fighter Wing at "Fursty" (the Americans' nickname for Fürstenfeldbruck), was renamed the 36th Fighter Bomber Wing (FBW) on 20 January 1950, receiving at this time the Republic F-84 Thunderjet of which the "Skyblazers" received four, in September the same year.

On 21 May 1952, Captain John P. O'Brien (the solo replacement) was killed at RAF Manston, In Great Britain, when his engine blew up during a low altitude pass.

By the following summer, the "Skyblazers" of the 36th FBW had already taken part in more than 260 air shows in twelve European countries. After the Manston accident, the team ceased its displays in August 1952. The USAFE then placed the "Skyblazers" under the responsibility of the 86th FBW equipped with the F-84E Thunderjet and based at Neubiberg, in Germany.

In October 1953, the team was placed under the authority of the 48th FBW based at Chaumont, in France, and equipped with the F-84G. In 1954, the 48th replaced its Thunderjets with the F-86F Sabre, planes which were then logically flown by the "Skyblazers" who used them during the 1955 and 1956 seasons.

The team moved once more to Bitburg in October 1956 and was placed under the authority of the 36th FBW, redesignated the 36th Fighter Day Wing. The whole of the Wing was equipped with the F-100C, and this naturally included the "Skyblazers", but the team had already begun flying with seven of these specially decorated planes the previous month.

At the end of the 1960 season, the From the end of the 1960 season, the Skyblazers' days were numbered, and the USAFE officially disbanded the team in January 1962.

"Skyblazers" Lockheed F-80B Shooting Star. Fürstenfeldbruck AB (Germany), 1949.

"Skyblazers" Republic F-84G Thunderjet. Fürstenfeldbruck AB, 1952.

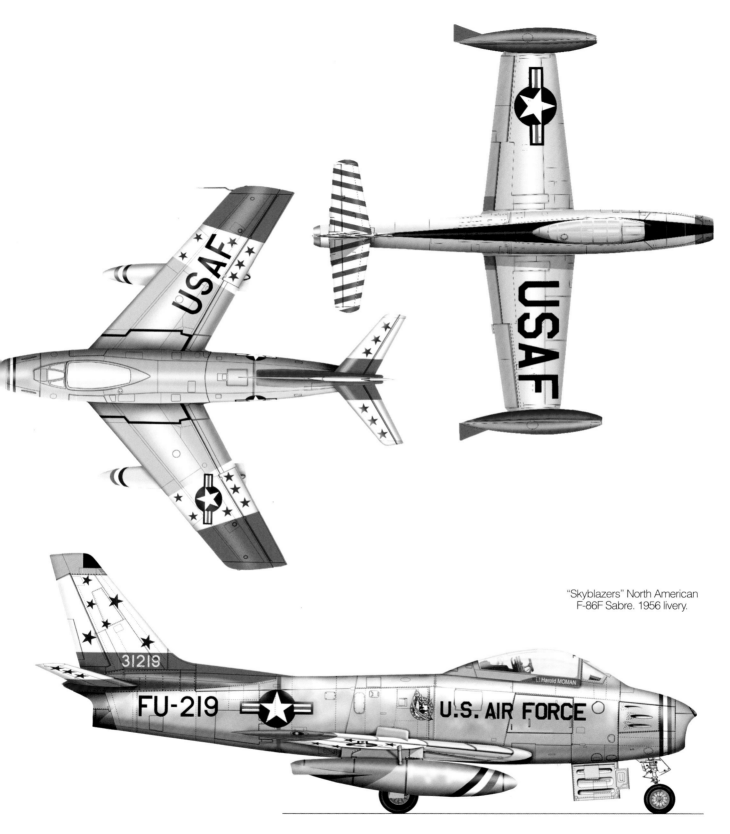

"Skyblazers" North American
F-86F Sabre. 1956 livery.

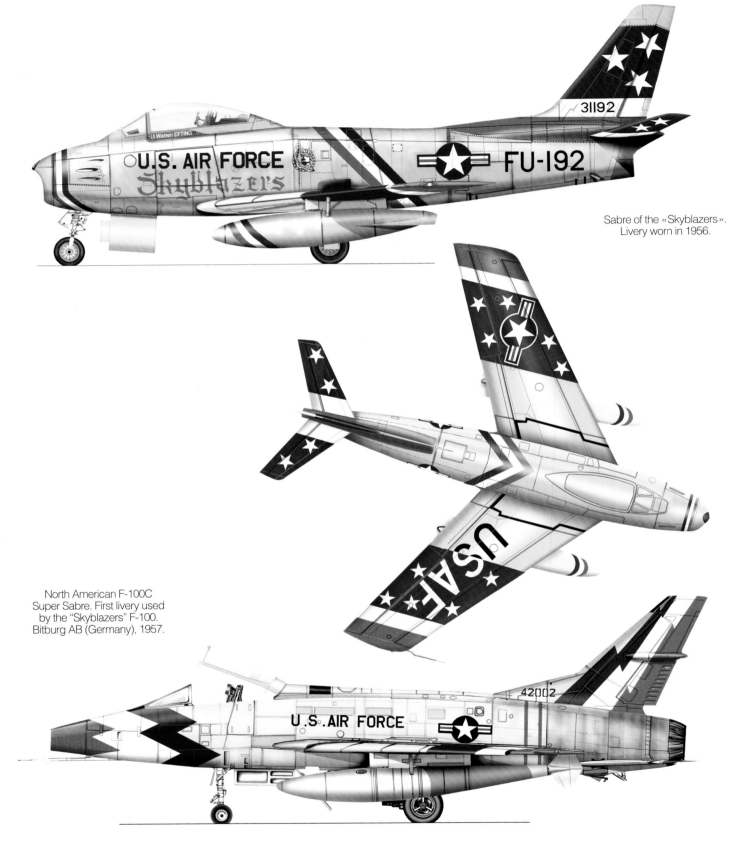

Sabre of the «Skyblazers».
Livery worn in 1956.

North American F-100C
Super Sabre. First livery used
by the "Skyblazers" F-100.
Bitburg AB (Germany), 1957.

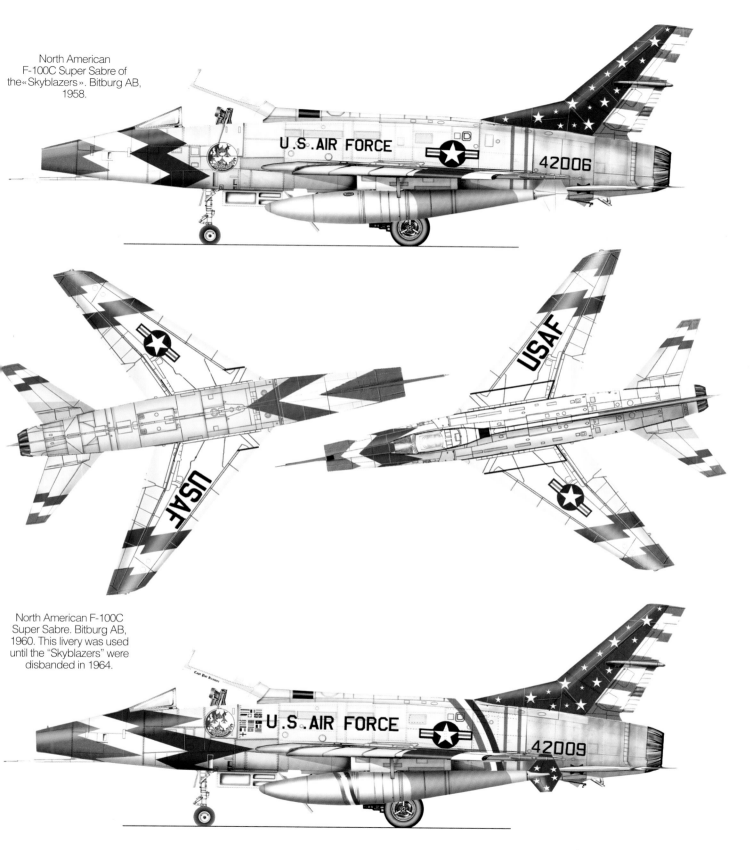

North American
F-100C Super Sabre of
the «Skyblazers». Bitburg AB,
1958.

North American F-100C
Super Sabre. Bitburg AB,
1960. This livery was used
until the "Skyblazers" were
disbanded in 1964.

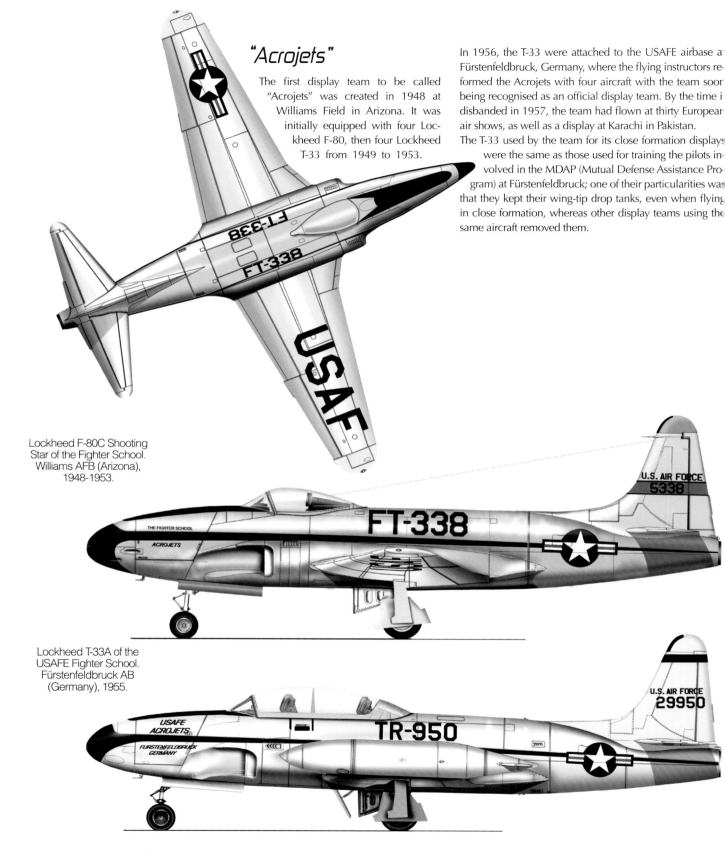

"Acrojets"

The first display team to be called "Acrojets" was created in 1948 at Williams Field in Arizona. It was initially equipped with four Lockheed F-80, then four Lockheed T-33 from 1949 to 1953.

In 1956, the T-33 were attached to the USAFE airbase at Fürstenfeldbruck, Germany, where the flying instructors re-formed the Acrojets with four aircraft with the team soon being recognised as an official display team. By the time it disbanded in 1957, the team had flown at thirty European air shows, as well as a display at Karachi in Pakistan.

The T-33 used by the team for its close formation displays were the same as those used for training the pilots involved in the MDAP (Mutual Defense Assistance Program) at Fürstenfeldbruck; one of their particularities was that they kept their wing-tip drop tanks, even when flying in close formation, whereas other display teams using the same aircraft removed them.

Lockheed F-80C Shooting Star of the Fighter School. Williams AFB (Arizona), 1948-1953.

Lockheed T-33A of the USAFE Fighter School. Fürstenfeldbruck AB (Germany), 1955.

"The Sabre Knights"

Formed in 1952 at the Hamilton air base in California, the "Sabre Knights" display team first used the North American F-86E and F Sabre which it later replaced with four F-86D Sabre Dog, thus becoming the only team to use this aircraft. The team's pilots normally belonged to the 325th FIS (Fighter Interceptor Squadron) of Air Defense Command, and flew part-time for the team. The team's leader, Lieutenant-Colonel Vince Gor-

don, was also a Second World War veteran and commanded a squadron; he was also a former member of the "Skyblazers". It was Gordon who formed the "Sabre Knights", the Air Defense Command's sole official team, shortly after having been attached to Hamilton, In August 1952.

The "Sabre Knights" accumulated 7,000 flying hours throughout their career and flew displays all over the United States. They were disbanded along with the 325th FIS in August 1955.

North American F-86F Sabre
of the 84th Fighter Interceptor
Squadron. Hamilton AFB
(California), 1952.

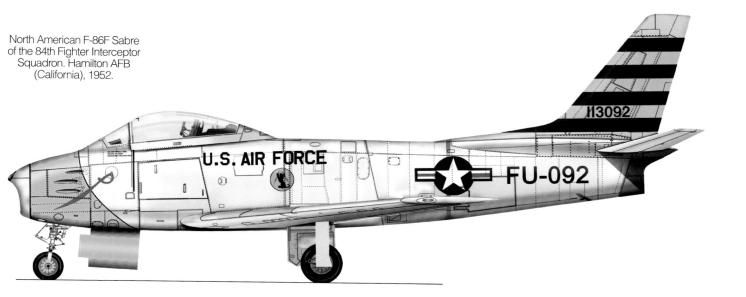

North American F-86E
Sabre of the 325th Fighter
Interceptor Squadron, 566th
TFW. Hamilton AFB,
October 1953.

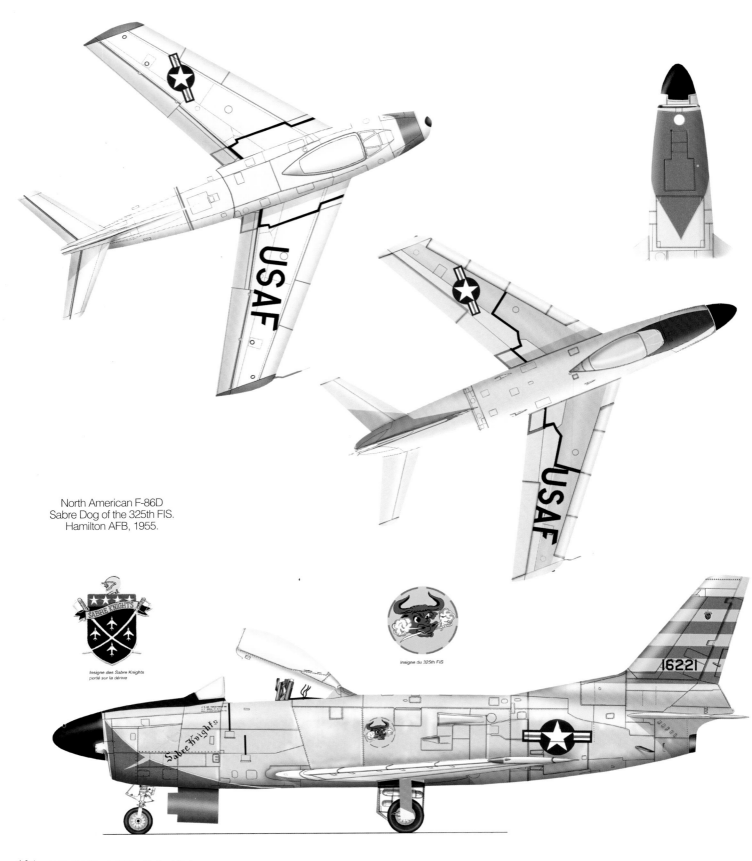

North American F-86D
Sabre Dog of the 325th FIS.
Hamilton AFB, 1955.

Insigne des Sabre Knights
porté sur la dérive

Insigne du 325th FIS

Sabre Knights

16221

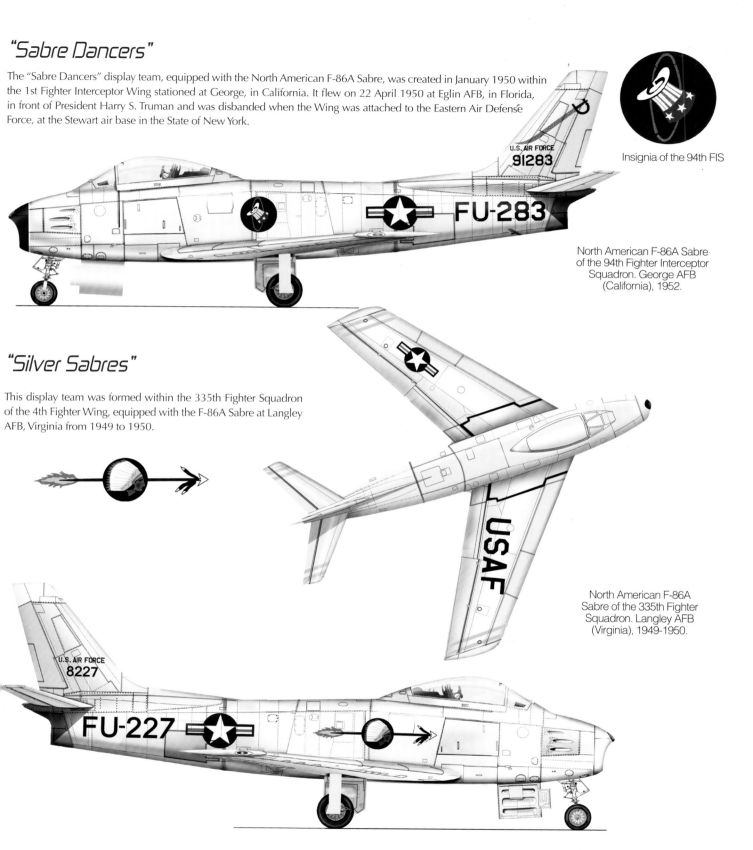

"Sabre Dancers"

The "Sabre Dancers" display team, equipped with the North American F-86A Sabre, was created in January 1950 within the 1st Fighter Interceptor Wing stationed at George, in California. It flew on 22 April 1950 at Eglin AFB, in Florida, in front of President Harry S. Truman and was disbanded when the Wing was attached to the Eastern Air Defense Force, at the Stewart air base in the State of New York.

Insignia of the 94th FIS

North American F-86A Sabre of the 94th Fighter Interceptor Squadron. George AFB (California), 1952.

"Silver Sabres"

This display team was formed within the 335th Fighter Squadron of the 4th Fighter Wing, equipped with the F-86A Sabre at Langley AFB, Virginia from 1949 to 1950.

North American F-86A Sabre of the 335th Fighter Squadron. Langley AFB (Virginia), 1949-1950.

"The Thunderbirds"

The USAF 3600th Aerobatic Squadron was created on 1 June 1953 and based at Luke in Arizona with four Republic F-84G Thunderjets. In the beginning, the squadron was given the name of "Stardusters", a name which was quickly changed to "Thunderbirds" due to the strong Indian culture of the south-east of the United States where the team was based.

A week after their creation, the "Thunderbirds" flew their first display over Luke AFB and at the beginning of the following year, they flew in South and Central America.

The first fatal accident occurred during a training flight on 13 December 1954, when one of the pilots was killed whilst flying a F-84G.

In 1955, the team was equipped with the Republic F-84F Thunderstreak and two more planes were added, bringing the total to six. The team flew one hundred displays throughout 1955.

Having moved to the Nellis air base in Nevada in 1956, the team was equipped with the North American F-100C Super Sabre, an aircraft that it would use for fourteen years.

This period was marked by several fatal accidents. On 26 September 1957, a pilot was killed whilst training on his F-100C at Nellis. 9 October 1958 was a black day for the "T-birds". The team's transport plane, a Fairchild C-123 Provider, was flying to an air show, carrying the technical personnel as well as passengers, when it crashed near Boise, Ohio, killing fourteen "Thunderbirds" personnel.

In December 1959 the team received F-100D with in-flight refuelling capability, allowing it to fly far afield, notably in the Far east where it gave twenty-nine displays. In 1963, the "Thunderbirds" flew in Europe and North Africa.

The following year, the team received the Republic F-105B Thunderchief and on 9 May1964, whilst giving a display over the Hamilton air base (California), aircraft n° 2, whilst climbing at 45°, suffered a structural problem. Its fuselage split in two at the weapons bay and the plane blew up, killing the pilot. In the wake of this accident, the F-105B needed important modifications made to its fuselage and the team went back to flying the F-100D.

In 1967, the "Thunderbirds" carried out their one-thousandth display and the following year were made the USAF's official display team.

In 1969, the Thunderbirds began flying the McDonnell Douglas F-4E Phantom II. There were two accidents concerning this aircraft in 1972, the first in June when a pilot was killed flying plane s/n 66-0321 and the second in December when the pilot and technician of plane s/n 67-0367 were killed during a test flight.

In 1974, the "T-Birds" adopted the Northrop T-38A Talon and, in the space of nine years, six pilots were killed in accidents with this type of plane. One of the most serious accidents happened on 18 January 1982 when, during a looping manoeuvre in a line the leader's plane encountered a technical problem, resulting in the collision of the four T-38A and the deaths of four pilots. This crash brought an end to the team's displays for eighteen months.

The team began flying displays again on 2 April 1983, after having moved on to the

General Dynamics F-16A Fighting Falcon.

It lost its first "Viper" (unofficial nickname of the F-16), plane n° 6, on 14 February 1994 at Indiana Springs Auxiliary Airfield, Nevada, when carrying out a spiral descent in training. The pilot survived, but this aerobatic manoeuvre was no longer carried out.

On 14 September 2003, during a display at Mountain Home AFB, Idaho, plane n° 6 suffered an engine failure after having made a dive manoeuvre. Its pilot tried in vain to control the aircraft and eventually managed to safely eject.

"The Thunderbirds" still fly today, equipped now with the F-16C, and use six aircraft, whether flying in the Unites States or on other continents.

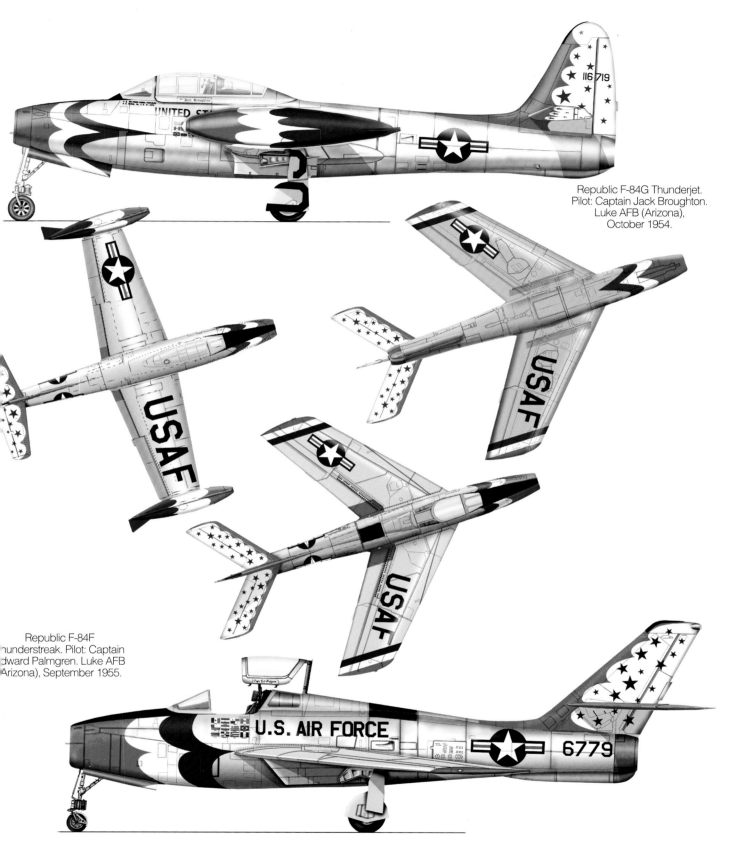

Republic F-84G Thunderjet.
Pilot: Captain Jack Broughton.
Luke AFB (Arizona),
October 1954.

Republic F-84F
Thunderstreak. Pilot: Captain
Edward Palmgren. Luke AFB
(Arizona), September 1955.

(USAF Photos)

U.S. AIR FORCE

52728

Insignia worn
on the port side.

Republic F-84F
Thunderstreak. Pilot: Captain
Edward Palmgren. Luke AFB
(Arizona), september 1955.

USAF

"Thunderbirds" NA F-100D
Super Sabre. 1964-1969
period.

U.S. AIR FORCE   FIVE

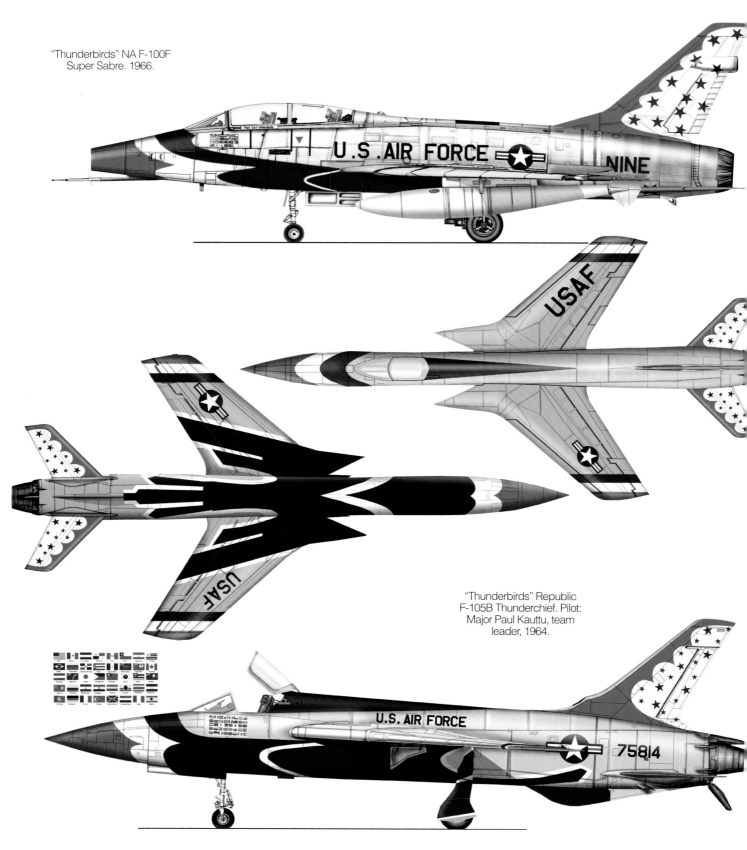

"Thunderbirds" NA F-100F
Super Sabre. 1966.

"Thunderbirds" Republic
F-105B Thunderchief. Pilot:
Major Paul Kauttu, team
leader, 1964.

(USAF)

Thunderbirds McDonnell
F-4E Phantom II. Nellis AFB
(Nevada). Aircraft n° 3, port
wingman in the diamond
formation. Seasons
1969 to 1973.

U.S. AIR FORCE

3

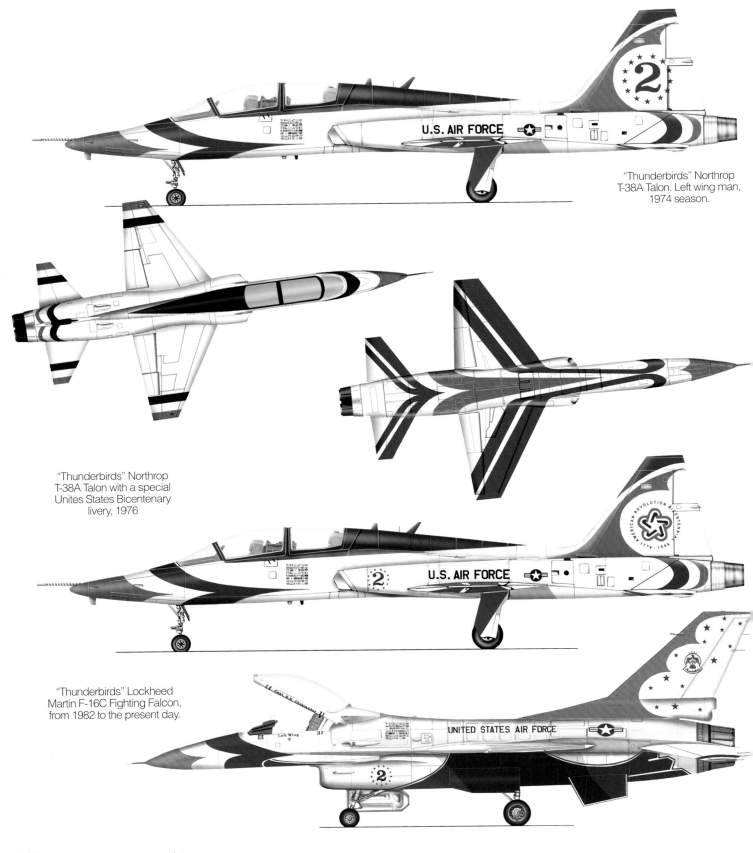

"Thunderbirds" Northrop
T-38A Talon. Left wing man,
1974 season.

"Thunderbirds" Northrop
T-38A Talon with a special
Unites States Bicentenary
livery, 1976

"Thunderbirds" Lockheed
Martin F-16C Fighting Falcon,
from 1982 to the present day.

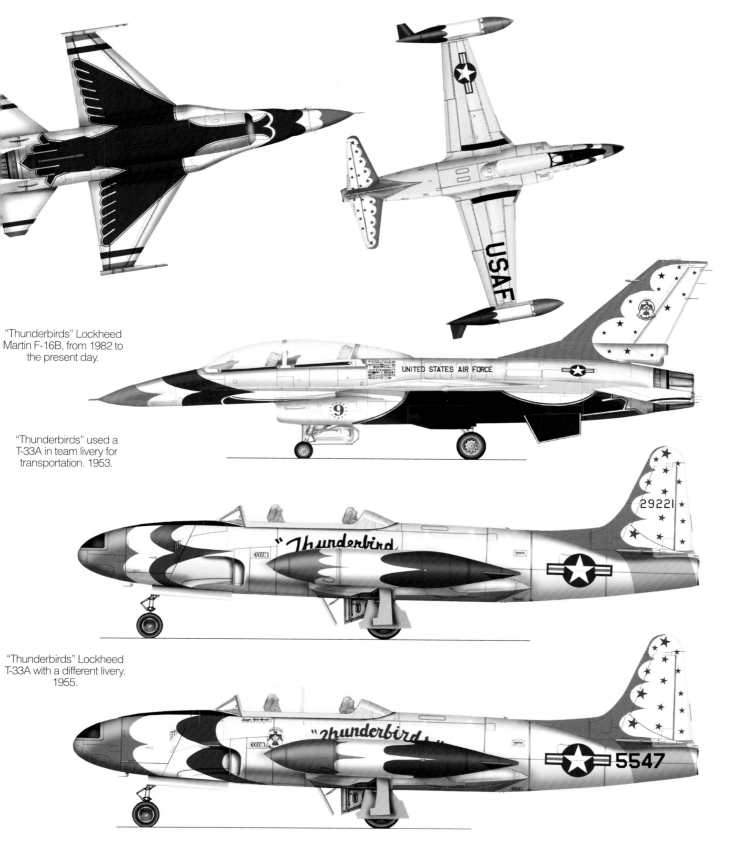

"Thunderbirds" Lockheed Martin F-16B, from 1982 to the present day.

"Thunderbirds" used a T-33A in team livery for transportation. 1953.

"Thunderbirds" Lockheed T-33A with a different livery. 1955.

"The Blue Angels"

The "Blue Angels" were created in April 1946 under the name of the US Navy Flight Demonstration Team. It comprised of five experienced pilots, all of whom had flown during the Second World War, and was equipped with the Grumman F6F-5 Hellcat. It flew its first public display on 15 June 1946 at Jacksonville, Florida, and in the following August, the team received the Grumman F8F-1 Bearcat.

In 1949, the team began flying jets with six Grumman F9F-2 Panthers, aircraft that it used until June 1950, when it stopped giving displays due to the outbreak of the Korean War.

Two years later, in 1952, the "Blue Angels", were reformed and set up base at Corpus Christi, Texas, with six F9F-5 Panthers. On 7 July 1952, two planes collided at low altitude during a display over their base. One of the pilots survived, but the other was killed when he ejected. During the course of the same 1952 season, two Vought F7U-1 Cutlass were added to the team's six Panthers, but they did not fly very often and were soon taken off the roster.

In 1953, the team received the Grumman F9F-6 Cougar (the swept-back wing version of the Panther), then the F9F-8 Cougar during the winter of 1954-1955. The "Blue Angels" went to Canada for the first time in 1956. During the four years flying with Cougars, the team lost four aircraft and two pilots.

In 1957, the team was equipped with the brand new Grumman F11F-1 Tiger which it used for eleven years and which allowed it to carry out new aerobatic manoeuvres. During the period of August 1958 to January 1968, the "Blue Angels" had fifteen accidents and seven of its pilots were killed.

At the end of 1968, the team adopted the McDonnell F-4J Phantom II. On 8 January 1972, one of these aircraft crashed into the ground whilst flying upside down at El Centro (California), killing the pilot, and on 8 March 1973, three other planes collided at Superstition Mountain (California), killing the three pilots. On 26 July 1973, while arriving at the Lakehurst NAS (New Jersey), two pilots and a chief mechanic in the navigator's seat, were killed when planes n°1 and n°4 collided, bringing a stop to the rest of the season.

In 1974, the "Blue Angels" took the official name of US Navy Flight Demonstration Squadron and began flying with the Douglas A-4F Skyhawk. In 1977, thirty years after their first display, the "Blue Angels" carried out their 2,000th display at Atlanta, Georgia. On 13 July 1985, two Skyhawks (n° 5 and n° 6) collided during a display at Niagara Falls (State of New York), whilst carrying out a looping manoeuvre. One of the pilots was killed, but the other managed to eject.

On 18 November 1986, the "Blue Angels" celebrated their 40th anniversary and presented their new plane, the McDonnel Douglas F/A-18A Hornet, and two twin-seater planes (F/A-18B) were added to the team. The team flew its 3,000th display on 7 September 1990. Between February 1987 and April 2007, five Hornets have been lost and three pilots killed, two of whom were flying a twin-seater. The "Blue Angels" are still flying and are equipped with the F/A-18C Hornet.

1982 season Blue Angels personnel pose alongside John Travolta and Olivia Newton-John, the stars at the time, of the movie «Grease». *(USN)*

The Grumman F8F Bearcat was the second mount of the Blue Angels and the last piston-engined aicraft used by the team, from 1946 to 1949.

"Blue Angels" Grumman
F-9F-2 Panther. 1951-1952.

The Blue Angels flew two F7U-1 Cutlasses as a side act during their 1953 show season in an effort to promote the new aircraft, but did not use them as part of their regular formation act. Both the pilots and ground crews found the aircraft generally unsatisfactory and it was apparent that the type was still experiencing teething troubles.

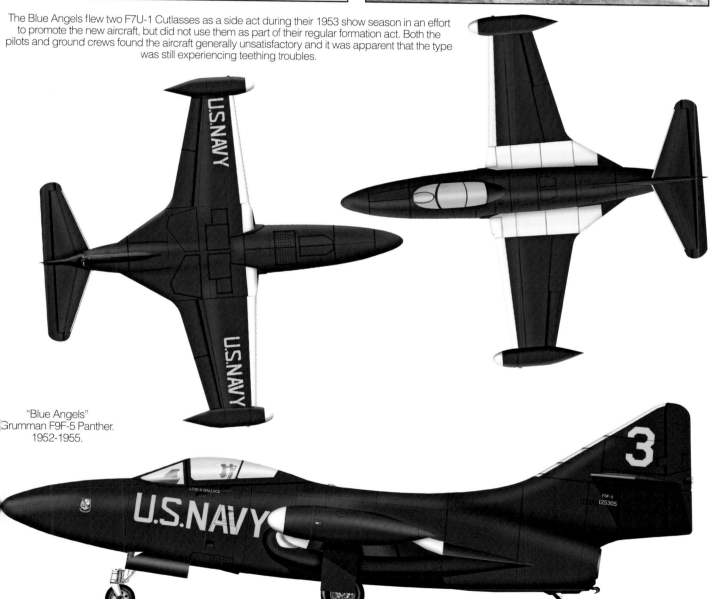

"Blue Angels"
Grumman F9F-5 Panther.
1952-1955.

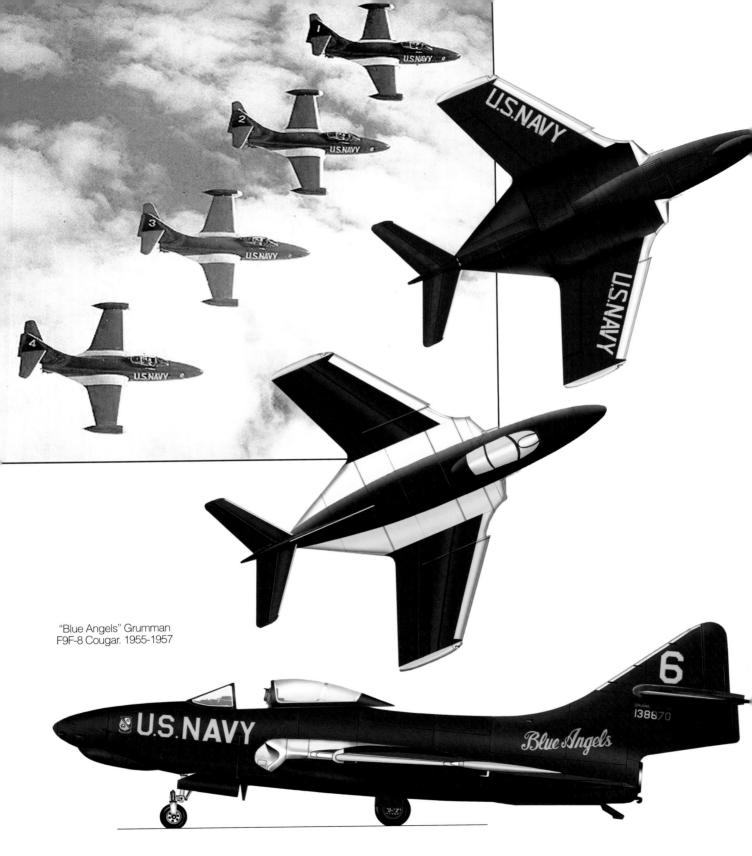

"Blue Angels" Grumman
F9F-8 Cougar. 1955-1957

Grumman F9F-8T Cougar, 1957-1969. This plane was used by the team, usually for transporting the commentator.

"Blue Angels" Grumman 11F-1 Tiger. Pilot: Lieutenant Hal Loney, 1968.

"Fat Albert", Blue Angels' C-130T Hercules support aircraft takes off dramatically, assisted by JATO rockets. The plane wears a livery similar to those of the other aircraft of the team. The JATO demonstration ended in 2009 due to dwindling supplies of rockets. *(USN)*

"Blue Angels" McDonnell-Douglas F-4J Phantom II. 1969-1973.

"Blue Angels" Douglas A-4F Skyhawk. 1969-1987.

Douglas TA-4J Skyhawk. "Blue Angels" support and communication aircraft, 1981 season.

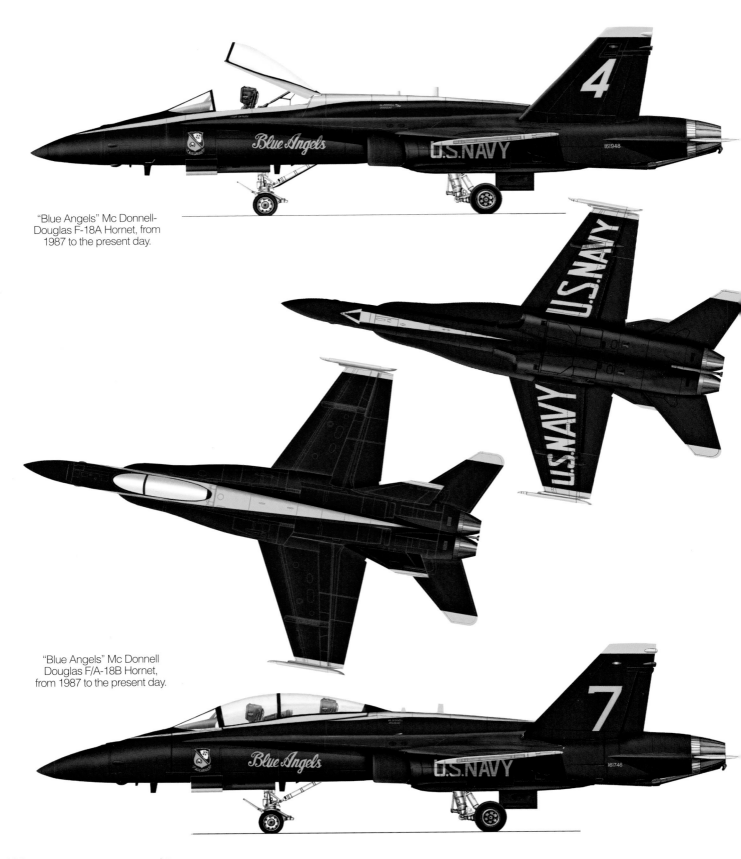

"Blue Angels" Mc Donnell-Douglas F-18A Hornet, from 1987 to the present day.

"Blue Angels" Mc Donnell Douglas F/A-18B Hornet, from 1987 to the present day.

Lockheed TV-1 Seastar.
The "Blue Angels", transport
plane, 1952 season.

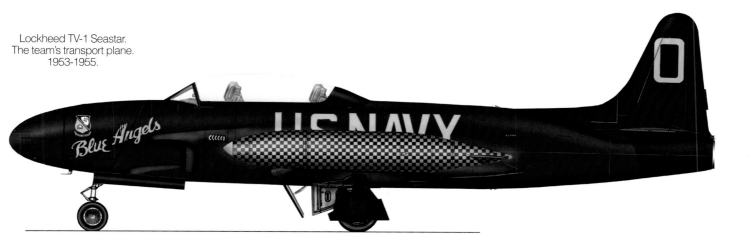

Lockheed TV-1 Seastar.
The team's transport plane.
1953-1955.

"Blue Angels" Lockheed TV-1
Seastar. 1956-1957.

YUGOSLAVIA

Akro Grupa 204

In 1959, the Jugoslovensko *Ratno Vazduhoplovstvo* (JRV, Yugoslavian Air Force) was equipped with the Canadair CL-13 Sabre Mk 4 (Canadian version of the F-86E built under licence) and in 1960, an unofficial display team was created, carrying out its first display at Zemun airport, Belgrade. This team later adopted the name of "Akro Grupa 204" and flew until 1965.

HUNGARY

CROATIA   ROMANIA

BOSNIA-H

YUGOSLAVIA

BULGARIA

MACEDONIA

ALBANIA

North American F-86E Sabre
of the "Akro Grupa 204"
display team, *Jugoslovensko
Ratno Vazduhoplovstvo*
(Yugoslavian Air Force).
Batajnica, 1960.

SUMMARY

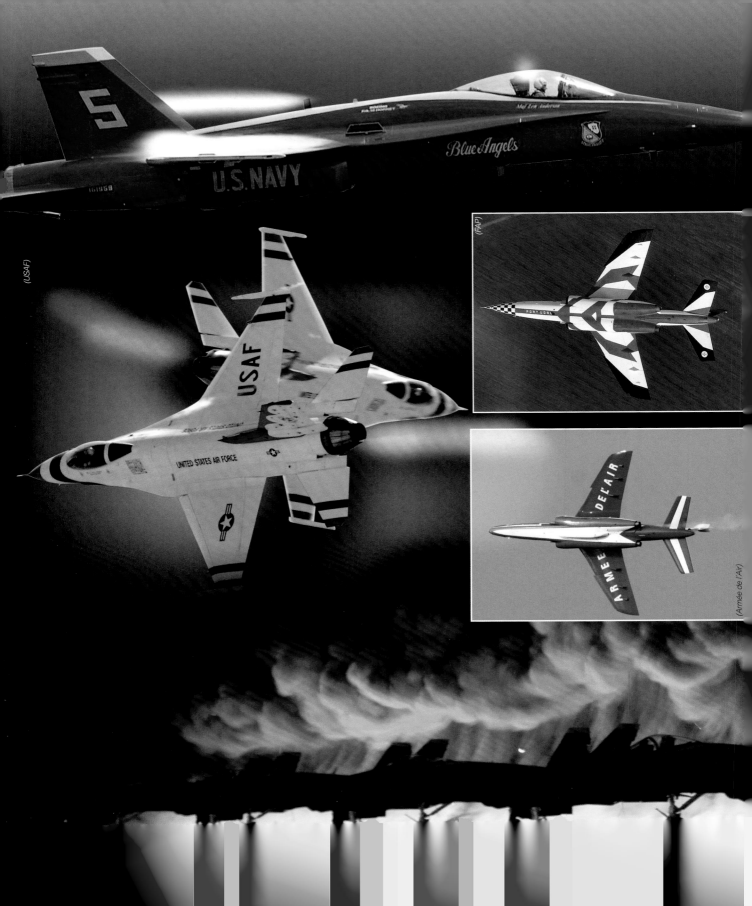

présente AVIONS ET PILOTES   presents PLANES AND PILOTS

N° 1. *Avions et Pilotes*
Le Messerschmitt 109,
1936-1942. Tome I

N° 2. *Avions et Pilotes*
Le Messerschmitt 109,
1942-1945. Tome II

N° 3. *Avions et Pilotes*
Le Curtiss P-40
1939-1945

N° 4. *Avions et Pilotes*
Le Junkers Ju 87
Stuka1936-1945

N° 1. *Planes and Pilots*
The Messerschmitt 109,
1936-1942. Volume I

N° 2. *Planes and Pilots*
The Messerschmitt 109,
1942-1945. Volume II

N° 3. *Planes and Pilots*
The Curtiss P-40
1939-1945

N° 5. *Avions et Pilotes*
Le North American P-51
Mustang, 1940-1980

N° 6. *Avions et Pilotes*
Le Mirage III
1955-2000

N° 8. *Avions et Pilotes*
L'aviation française
1939-1942. Tome II

N° 9. *Avions et Pilotes*
Le Focke Wulf
FW 190 1940-1945

N° 4. *Planes and Pilots*
The Junkers Ju 87
Stuka1936-1945

N° 5. *Planes and Pilots*
The North American P-51
Mustang, 1940-1980

N° 6. *Planes and Pilots*
The French Mirage III
1955-2000

N° 10. *Avions et Pilotes*
Le F-4 Phantom
US Navy et USMC

N° 11. *Avions et Pilotes*
Les chasseurs bimoteurs
Messerschmitt
1939-1945

N° 12. *Avions et Pilotes*
Le MIG21
Fishbed, 1955-2010

N° 13. *Avions et Pilotes*
Le F-4 Phantom
US Air Force et les
versions d'exportations.
Tome II

N° 8. *Planes and Pilots*
French aircraft
1939-1942. Volume II

N° 9. *Planes and Pilots*
The Focke Wulf FW 190
1940-1945

N° 10. *Planes and Pilots*
The F-4 Phantom
US Navy and USMC
Volume I

LES MATÉRIELS DE L'ARMÉE DE L'AIR (only in French)

N° 1. *Armée de l'air*
MD 450 Ouragan
1947-1960

N° 2. *Armée de l'air*
Sepecat Jaguar
1965-2000

N° 3. *Armée de l'air*
Mirage F1C et F1B
1973-2003

N° 4. *Armée de l'air*
P-47 Thunderbolt
1943-1962

N° 11. *Planes and Pilots*
Messerschmitt's
twin-engined fighters
1939-1945

N° 12. *Planes and Pilots*
The MIG 21

N° 13. *Planes and Pilots*
The F-4 Phantom
USAF and exports
versions. Volume II

N° 5. *Armée de l'air*
GAMD Mirage IV
1959-2005

N° 6. *Armée de l'air*
Mirage F1CR et F1 CT
1973-2003

N° 7. *Armée de l'air*
C-160 Transall
1967-2008

N° 8. *Armée de l'air*
GAMD Mirage III. Tome I
1955-2000

N° 9. *Armée de l'air*
GAMD Mirage III & 5.
Tome II. 1955-2000

LES AVIONS DE COMBAT AMÉRICAINS
GREAT AMERICAN COMBAT AIRCRAFT

N° 1. *Avions de combat américains*
F-14 Tomcat,
1974-2006

N° 2. *Avions de combat américains*
F-16 Tome I
Fighting Falcon
Versions A et B.

L'AVENTURE AÉRIENNE CHEZ **HISTOIRE & COLLECTIONS**
AIR STORIES FROM **HISTOIRE & COLLECTIONS**

Dans la collection : «LÉGENDES DU CIEL»
In the collection:"LEGEND OF THE SKY"

Lockheed Constellation
De l'Excalibur au Starliner,
1945-1960
Format 23 x 31, 176 pages

Boeing 707 et KC-135
Les versions civiles et militaires,
1952-2008
Format 23 x 31, 208 pages

Lockheed Constellation
From Excalibur to Starliner,
1945-1960
176 pages

Boeing 707 and KC-135
Civilian and military versions,
1952-2008
208 pages

Dans la collection : A«LES GRANDS ILLUSTRATEURS»
In the collection:"THE ART OF…"

Le Corsair
L'aventure du flibustier, du
Pacifique à la guerre du Football
par B. Pautigny
Format 23 x 31, 128 pages

60 ans d'avions de combat
L'histoire de la guerre aérienne
par les profils de Bruno Pautigny
Format 23 x 31, 196 pages

L'art de Daniel Bechennec
Les plus belles illustrations
militaires de Daniel Béchennec
Format 23 x 31, 160 pages

Corsair
Over 150 profiles and dozes
of technical plates by B. Pautigny
128 pages

60 years of combat aircraft
Over 300 profiles
by Bruno Pautigny
196 pages

The Art of Daniel Bechennec
The famous French
military illustrator
160 pages

Dans la collection :
«HISTOIRES AÉRIENNES»
In the collection: "AIR STORIES"

La 5th Air Force
La chasse et le bombardement
dans le Pacifique Sud
Format 21 x 25, 112 pages

5th Air Force
Fighting and Bombing Squadrons
over South Pacific
112 pages

Dans la collection : «LES GRANDES UNITÉS» In the collection: "GREAT ARMY AIR FORCES"

La 8th Air Force
Le bombardement stratégique
en Europe, 1942-1945
Format 23 x 31, 192 pages

8th Air Force
The missions flown by B-17 crews
over the Reich, 1942-1945
192 pages

La 9th Air Force
Le bombardement tactique
en Europe, 1942-1945
Format 23 x 31, 192 pages

9th Air Force
Tactical aviation over Europe,
1942-1945
192 pages

Curtiss H-75 au combat
Le groupe de Chasse 1/5
dans la campagne de France
1939-1940
Format 23 x 31, 144 pages

trouvez le catalogue intégral de nos publications sur *(Online catalog)* www.histoireetcollections.fr

Edited by Dominique Breffort. Design and layout by Magali Masselin.

ISBN: 978-2-35250-168-8

Publisher's number: 35250

© Histoire & Collections 2010

SA au capital de 182 938,82 €

5, avenue de la République
F-75541 Paris Cédex 11 - FRANCE

Tel: +33-1 40 21 18 20 / Fax: +33-1 47 00 51 11

w w w . h i s t o i r e e t c o l l e c t i o n s . f r

This book has been designed, typed, laid-out and processed by *Histoire & Collections* on fully integrated computer equipment.

Color separation: *Studio A&C*

Print by *MCC GRAPHICS - ELKAR*, Spain, European Union.

November 2010